TURNER **CLASSIC** MOVIES.

MOVIE NIGHT

Menus

DINNER AND DRINK RECIPES
INSPIRED BY FILMS WE LOVE

Tenaya Darlington and
André Darlington

RUNNING PRESS
PHILADELPHIA · LONDON

Published by Running Press,
An Imprint of Perseus Books, LLC.,
A Subsidiary of Hachette Book Group, Inc.

Books published by Running Press are available at special discounts for bulk purchases
in the United States by corporations, institutions, and other organizations. For more
information, please contact the Special Markets Department at the Perseus Books Group,
2300 Chestnut Street, Suite 200, Philadelphia, PA 19103, or call (800) 810-4145,
ext. 5000, or e-mail special.markets@perseusbooks.com.

ISBN 978-0-7624-6093-9
Library of Congress Control Number: 2016947726

E-book ISBN 978-0-7624-6116-5

9 8 7 6 5 4 3 2 1
Digit on the right indicates the number of this printing

Edited by Cindy De La Hoz
Designed by Susan Van Horn
Food and prop styling by Carrie Purcell
Typography: Brandon, Flama, Cervo, and Wisdom Script

Running Press Book Publishers
2300 Chestnut Street
Philadelphia, PA 19103-4371

Visit us on the web!
www.offthemenublog.com
www.tcm.com

Contents

TAKE THREE:
SPECIAL OCCASIONS AND RESOURCES—*page 239*

TAKE ONE
Introduction

"Good movies make you care, make you believe in possibilities again."—PAULINE KAEL

HELLO, GORGEOUS. Sit down and have a drink with us. We've been expecting you. After all, what's more enticing than a cocktail and a movie, with a meal to match the mood?

We began pairing drinks and movies a few years ago, just as we were polishing the pages of a manuscript about classic and modern mixed drinks for our first book together, *The New Cocktail Hour*. In the process of our (ahem) research, we ran across dozens of recipes named after early Hollywood stars, like Mary Pickford and Douglas Fairbanks. They piqued our curiosity, and so, naturally, we broke out our shakers, fixed ourselves a pair of ethereal drinks in frosty coupes, and sat down to watch America's first star couple. Although we have always loved film—as siblings, we watched many movies together—we did not have a strong grasp of early Hollywood, or the extent of its extravagant cocktail culture.

What we saw in the flickering faces on screen was so enthralling, we began searching for more excuses to mix spirits and movies. We devoured *The Thin Man* series with its regal parties and delighted in smoky-voiced Greta Garbo, whose first words on film were a "give me a viskey." That's how the book in your hands came to be; as we discovered cocktails named after actors or films—or mentioned in scenes—we hosted our own dinner-and-a-movie nights with drinks. Little did we know that we'd find so many films featuring classic cocktails and such inspired home entertaining, from the fashion-fabulous soirees peppered throughout the films of the 1930s and '40s, to the sensual nightcap served in *The Graduate* (1967) and the celebratory Champagne Cocktail prepared in *Moonstruck* (1987).

This book highlights some of the greatest dining and drinking scenes to appear on screen from the 1930s to the mid-1980s. We watched hundreds of films in order to curate this list, and there were many we were sorry to leave out. For a title to make it into these pages, it needed to have rousing food and drink scenes. And we had to love it—we had to imagine ourselves making it the centerpiece of an entire meal to share with friends. From there, we created a menu inspired by each movie.

If you've ever wanted to learn how to fix a well-balanced Manhattan or Martini, we'll show you how. In the meantime, invite your besties over for a special evening—or pick a movie night menu for your next family bash. Look for our lists of Special Occasion movies (page 239) in back, along with tips on great date-night films that are perfect for two. Then, settle in for glamour, great laughs, and some of the most glorious drinks and snacks of your lives. May you enjoy many starry-eyed evenings.

How to Throw a Movie Party

When we host, we love to drop a cocktail into people's hands as soon as they take off their coats. Then we'll set out some snacks, start a movie, and let dinner bubble on the stove or sizzle on the grill. Depending on the film, we'll serve a meal on the coffee table while everyone's watching, or we'll press pause and send our guests to the table for a candle-lit interlude.

In this book, we offer lots of ideas about how to make these evenings special, from table settings to suggested wines. Relax, take it easy, and let these meals flow naturally. The most important thing is that you enjoy yourself and the films. The menus are fairly simple, and none of them require hideous amounts of prep. For each menu, you'll find:

★ **Movie notes that offer background on each film**

★ **Recipes for dishes that are prepared in or are inspired by the film**

★ **"While You're Watching" sidebars (think: fun trivia or hidden details)**

★ **"Set the Scene" tips to help you round out a theme party**

Whether you're a movie buff or just beginning to delve into American cinema, we hope you'll find the organization of this book useful. We kept the movies in chronological order, after much debate, because we love to study the evolution of culture. By sipping and screening your way through these pages, you can observe fascinating changes in fashion, home décor, social customs, career choices, entertaining, music, modes of travel, politics, and personal style.

Whatever your interests, we invite you to seek out your own patterns in these thirty films. Cheers, and happy viewing!

Shake and Stir Like a Star

Fixing a cocktail doesn't require a lot of fancy equipment. You can start with a mason jar for shaking and stirring, or up your game with a Boston shaker—the professional bartender's tool. It comes with two parts: a 16-ounce mixing glass or pint glass, plus a 24-ounce shaker tin. It's simpler in design than the iconic three-piece shaker, which can be difficult to pull apart when it gets cold. If you have a beloved vintage shaker, though, by all means use it.

Here are some tips to help you make beautiful cocktails:

★ **Start with fresh ice.** Old ice can pick up the taste of your freezer and result in off flavors. Use filtered water and try making ice in silicone ice trays—they're the cocktailer's best friend. The ice pops out easily, and you can fashion large cubes or small. Those impressive large cubes of ice? They have a real purpose: they melt slowly, resulting in a less watery drink. (We love to use them for Manhattans.)

★ **Use quality ingredients.** Freshly squeezed citrus tastes better than bottled juices. Batch your juices a few hours before the party if you're entertaining a crowd.

★ **Stir spirits-only drinks.** Manhattans and Martinis? Don't shake 'em, no matter what you see on screen! Stir them—melting the ice a bit and blending the spirits gently. A 20- to 30-second stir is just about right for yielding a dilution ratio that is ¼ water. This will ensure that your drink is ice cold and well balanced in flavor. To stir a drink, you can pour the spirits into the bottom half of your shaker and stir with a long bar spoon. Then, strain the cocktail into a prepared glass.

★ **Shake any drink with citrus, cream, eggs, and/or muddled ingredients.** Shaking a drink helps these ingredients meld with spirits. When using whole egg or egg white (see note on page 10), you first "dry shake" the ingredients to emulsify them, then add ice and shake a second time. The goal is for your cocktail to reach the same temperature as the ice—generally 12 to 15 seconds of shaking.

★ **Chill (or warm) your glassware.** Pouring a well-stirred martini into a chilled coupe or martini glass not only looks glamorous, but it keeps your drink cold longer. For drinks served on the rocks, a chilled glass helps prevent the ice from melting quickly and rendering the drink watery. Pop your glasses into the freezer for about 15 minutes and you'll have frosty glasses. Obviously, if you're making a hot drink, you'll want to use a warm glass—best achieved by filling a mug with boiled water.

★ **Don't skip the garnishes.** A stunning cocktail garnish is an aesthetic creation—the feather on a hat. A well-prepared garnish—some freshly grated nutmeg, a citrus twist, or a sprig of fresh herbs—not only enhances the look of the drink, it's also the first aroma that rises from the glass. If a drink calls for a twist of citrus peel—a common garnish in this book—you'll want to use a paring knife or Y-peeler to remove a swath of the rind (2 to 3 inches long), avoiding as much white pith as possible. When you twist the peel over the drink, you express citrus oil, creating a lovely mist. Run the squeezed peel around the lip of the glass, then drop the peel into the drink or rest the peel on the edge.

Congratulations! You are now ready to prepare a great cocktail.

On Eggs and Egg Cocktails

You'll find several egg-based cocktails in this book, and they are wonderful—rich and frothy, a sensation among early drink lovers who encountered flips, nogs, and fizzes at the finest saloons during the Golden Age of cocktails (1860s to Prohibition). We're required to tell you that because of the slight risk of salmonella, raw eggs should not be served to the very young, the ill or elderly, or to pregnant women. If you're concerned about raw egg, use pasteurized whites. Generally, we look for the freshest, highest-quality eggs we can find at a farmers' market. We wash them well, and make sure to avoid dropping any shell into our shakers.

Simple Syrup

When a recipe calls for simple syrup, just combine 1 part warm water to 1 part granulated sugar. No need to boil this syrup on the stove. We make it in a jar so it's easy to shake; the sugar doesn't take long to dissolve. Store the mixture in the fridge so it's cold when you need it for cocktails.

TAKE TWO

Movie Menus

THE DIVORCÉE (1930)

Menu

DESSERT WITH FRIENDS

Clover Club Cocktail

Beet Red Devil Cake with Chocolate Frosting

N ORMA SHEARER FOUGHT FOR THE RIGHT TO PLAY THE SWEET but sexually provocative Jerry Martin in this 1930 film from MGM, and she works the camera like a spider on a fly. Every look is searing, every costume change sensational. This kind of movie will make the ladies want to revert to flapperdom and refashion an entire apartment with art deco touches—every light fixture, every vase drips with style. Shearer, the "good girl" star of films dating back to 1919, wasn't perceived as sexy, so to win her part, she hired photographer George Hurrell to help her develop a simmering look. When Shearer showed Irving Thalberg (her hubby and the production chief of MGM) some sample shots of her lounging in low-cut gowns, he was amazed. He handed her the role, and she won an Oscar.

Based on the taboo-busting novel *Ex-Wife*, *The Divorcée* dissects marital double standards, a popular topic after the suffragist movement in the 1920s. When Jerry's husband, Ted (Chester Morris), cheats on her, she evens the score by doing the same with his close friend. And so the duplicity begins. Party scene after party scene unfolds with Jerry and her ex dancing and drinking, chasing and being chased. It's worth noting that *The Divorcée* appeared just after the stock market crash of 1929 had devastated Americans and Hollywood was charged with keeping spirits high. Prohibition was still in effect, and movie censorship czar Will Hays was stumping to keep debauchery off screens (though his crusade would not prove successful until a few years later). Films like *The Divorcée* captured the spirit of the times, when vices and vamps were on everyone's minds. Here, as in so many films of the "Pre-Code Era" before censorship was strictly enforced, a strong female lead embodies the zeitgeist.

Opposite: **Norma Shearer, Robert Montgomery, George Irving, and Chester Morris**

Don't even try to keep up with all the cocktails that appear on screen. A single Clover Club will do: a decadent pre-Prohibition creation made with raspberry syrup and feathery egg white. It's a perfect pairing for the plush design sensibility evident throughout *The Divorcée*.

SEX AND PRE-CODE FILMS

With its overt exploration of divorce and infidelity, *The Divorcée* is an example of pre-code Hollywood at its finest. It was made before the Production Code Administration won its fight to enforce a rigid list of censorship guidelines in 1934. Sexually suggestive movies provoked outrage from religious groups, who threatened to boycott movie theaters. A purification of cinema was called for, and producers proceeded to strip scripts of "lustful kissing" and other potentially sinful acts. The Production Code, drafted by Father Daniel Lord, a Jesuit priest, influenced the creative direction of movies from roughly 1934 through the 1960s, until it was finally dismantled in 1968 and replaced by a rating system.

Curious to check out other notable pre-code films? Look for *Night Nurse* (1931), *Red-Headed Woman* (1932), and *She Done Him Wrong* (1933). Sassy and sometimes downright strange, these films have garnered a cult following, in part due to their strong female leads. *Female* (page 29) is another great example.

Set the Scene ◄◄◄◄◄◄

Confetti and balloons fill the screen. This movie is full of weddings, dinner parties, and card games. Play some crackly Jazz-Age records (we love trumpeter Bunny Berigan or Hot Lips Page), and break out your knee-length skirts and tweed vests. Despite the film's title, it's a darkly charming movie. We like to show it on New Year's Eve.

While You're Watching…

★ *The Divorcée* was based upon the novel *Ex-Wife*, which was considered so steamy that author Ursula Parrott published it anonymously.

★ Shearer's Oscar win for the role of Jerry was contentious. Many thought Garbo would and should win for *Anna Christie*, her first speaking role. Another great film from 1930, it's worth watching just to hear Garbo order a Whiskey Ginger in that smoky voice of hers.

Norma Shearer took on a sultry new look to win the role of Jerry Martin.

Clover Club Cocktail

Seductively frothy, the Clover Club is one of the most elegant drinks in the cocktail canon. It's crisp and bright, thanks to lemon and vermouth, and it exudes the smell and taste of just-picked raspberries. Despite being pink, it's hardly a lady's cocktail—it was invented by a men's club of the same name, which met in a downtown Philadelphia hotel starting in 1896. Note: We like to use a fresh organic egg, preferably from the farmers' market.

1½ ounces gin

½ ounce dry vermouth

½ ounce fresh lemon juice

½ ounce raspberry syrup (see recipe)

¾ ounce fresh egg white

Raspberries, for garnish

"Hello, Jerry. We were just drinking to your happiness."

—PAUL

Shake all of the ingredients without ice. This is called "dry-shaking," and it is a method used to ensure that the egg gets a frothy texture and incorporates fully with the other ingredients. Then, shake again with ice and strain into a chilled coupe glass. Garnish with skewered raspberries resting on the glass.

For raspberry syrup: Combine 1½ cups of fresh raspberries with ½ cup water and 1 cup granulated sugar in a medium-size bowl. Stir, macerating the berries with the back of your spoon. Cover the mixture, and let it rest on the counter for 8 to 12 hours, or overnight. Strain the mixture through a sieve using the back of a large spoon to press down on the berries and extract all the juices. Discard the solids. Transfer the syrup to a clean jar and refrigerate for up to a week. Note: This syrup is best used within a few days, when the aroma of fresh raspberries is most intense.

Beet Red Devil Cake with Chocolate Frosting

(PHOTO ON PAGE 16)

Cakes abound in The Divorcée, *from a chocolate layer cake served to revelers at a hunting lodge in the opening scene, to a wedding cake destroyed by a jealous husband. Here, we draw on a classic red devil cake, popular during the 1930s, but made extra moist by the addition of beets (rather than dye). This recipe is lightly adapted from* The Moosewood Restaurant Book of Desserts, *a staple in our house growing up. For a fanciful variation that pairs well with the Clover Club, we like to slather raspberry jam between the layers before enrobing this cake with chocolate frosting. Ours is a rich and creamy frosting that sets up quickly and is thick enough to pipe. This recipe makes plenty of frosting to cover a two-tier cake.*

SERVES 8

For the cake

1 can (15-ounce) sliced beets

3 large eggs

1½ cups granulated sugar

½ cup vegetable oil

2 teaspoons vanilla extract

½ teaspoon salt

1½ cups all-purpose white flour

¾ cup unsweetened cocoa powder

1½ teaspoons baking soda

Preheat the oven to 350°F. Butter and flour two 9-inch round cake pans.

In a blender, puree the beets along with ½ cup of their juice. Add eggs, and blend again until frothy. Pour the contents into a large mixing bowl and add sugar, oil, vanilla, and salt.

In a small bowl, whisk together flour, cocoa, and baking soda. Sift these dry ingredients into the egg mixture in four stages, mixing well between each addition.

Divide the batter between the two cake pans, and bake for 25 to 30 minutes, or until a toothpick inserted into the center comes out clean. Let the cakes cool, then run a butter knife around the edge of the pan and loosen them gently before inverting.

Tip: Freeze the cake layers for 10 minutes before frosting them. They'll be less likely to tear.

For the chocolate frosting

12 ounces bittersweet chocolate (three 4-ounce bars), chopped

1¾ cups (14 ounces) heavy cream

½ cup (4 ounces) sour cream

¼ teaspoon salt

Fresh raspberries (optional), for garnish

In the top part of a double boiler, warm the chocolate and heavy cream over gently simmering water. Stir until completely melted. Remove the pan from the heat and cool slightly (about 10 minutes). Add the sour cream and salt. Stir until combined.

Set the frosting aside until it reaches room temperature. Then, whisk or beat it with an electric mixer just until it thickens and turns a shade lighter in color.

To frost, be sure your cake is cool or chilled (see tip on page 18). Use a small spatula or butter knife to spread about 1 cup of the frosting evenly across the top of the first layer. Then, stack the second cake layer on top. Spread frosting evenly across the top and down the sides of both layers. Garnish with fresh raspberries, if desired.

Left: **Norma Shearer and Chester Morris embracing on their anniversary**

GRAND HOTEL (1932)

Menu

DINING AND DANCING

Louisiana Flip

German Pancake with Ham and Gruyère
or Berries and Cream

AN OPULENT ART DECO HOTEL IN BERLIN AND AN ALL-STAR CAST. Greta Garbo, Joan Crawford, brothers John Barrymore and Lionel Barrymore, and Wallace Beery all deliver magnetic performances in this Oscar-winning drama about five guests whose lives intertwine during their hotel stay. Producer Irving Thalberg worked magic during the dark years of the Depression, making *Grand Hotel* one of the first movies to feature an ensemble cast of high-power actors. This was something no director had done before, since investing so much star power in a single film was deemed risky. Luckily, *Grand Hotel* was a box office sensation. It won Best Picture and was later added to the National Film Registry.

Our menu is inspired by two of the movie's most dramatic characters, Lionel Barrymore and Greta Garbo. Barrymore plays Otto Kringelein, a sickly old man intent on spending his last days in luxury. He orders Louisiana Flips in the hotel's Yellow Room and tags along after the ladies, inviting anyone who will indulge him to enjoy Champagne and caviar in his royal suite. Garbo plays a Russian dancer, Grusinskaya, who swans about in satin gowns as ethereal as this meal's main course, a plush pancake that swings sweet or savory.

Lovers of vintage fashion, prepare to be swept away. This is one of our all-time favorite films—it's novel-like in scope, plus artfully shot and acted. It's also worth noting that the Barrymores, John and Lionel, are part of one of Hollywood's great acting families, of which Drew Barrymore is a descendent. In *Grand Hotel*, megastar John Barrymore plays the tragic figure of "the Baron," a master thief and seducer.

Opposite: **Jean Hersholt as Senf, the hotel porter**

The 1930s were an era of bias-cut dresses designed to hide thin, Depression-era figures, and film stars like Garbo and Crawford created a beautiful distraction from it all, despite presenting unattainable glamour. Play waltz music as guests arrive and serve everyone a round of flips. The tone of the film is formal, elegant—think tuxedos and white gloves. If you want to set up a bar cart and serve more than flips, include chilled Champagne and absinthe (which makes a lovely digestif called an Absinthe Frappé when shaken with a little simple syrup and served over crushed ice with a sprig of mint).

While You're Watching...

★ Crawford and Garbo never appear in the same frame. In other words, they were prevented from trying to upstage each other.

★ Listen for Garbo's famous line, "I want to be alone." It later became synonymous with her mysterious personality. She was an iconoclast who refused to marry.

★ The script for *Grand Hotel* was based on a bestselling book, *Menschen im Hotel* (1929), written by Viennese author Vicki Baum. During the late 1920s and early '30s, she lived in Berlin and wrote five serialized novels. *Grand Hotel* made her wildly famous, and she was marketed internationally as Weimar's "New Woman"—independent, fashionable, and athletic (she boxed).

Opposite: **Joan Crawford and Lionel Barrymore, enjoying his Louisiana Flip** | *Above:* **Greta Garbo reclining on a bed while her paramour, the Baron (John Barrymore), woos her**

"To life! To the magnificent, dangerous, brief, brief, wonderful life . . . and the courage to live it!"

—OTTO KRINGELEIN

Louisiana Flip

There's lots of speculation about this recipe, which has fallen through the cracks of Hollywood history. Otto Kringelein (Lionel Barrymore) attempts to order one for Flaemmchen (Joan Crawford), but she opts for absinthe instead. To be clear, a "flip" is a class of drinks that are made with whole egg, not unlike a nog (which contains both egg and cream). This particular drink is delightfully frothy and tastes a bit like a Creamsicle. If you want to play up the German theme of this film, serve this cocktail with pretzels.

2 ounces light rum

½ ounce triple sec

½ ounce fresh orange juice

2 teaspoons grenadine

1 small fresh egg

Freshly ground nutmeg, for garnish

Shake ingredients vigorously without ice. Add ice and reshake. Strain into a cocktail glass or flute. Garnish with ground nutmeg.

German Pancake with Ham and Gruyère or Berries and Cream

Like a giant popover, this dish emerges from the oven like a puffed-up parachute. Once it falls—and it will fall—cut it into quarters and serve it forth. For a crowd, we usually make several. They are easy to fix and quick to bake. Try making one that is savory, followed by one that is sweet (see tip below). The savory version is terrific served alongside an arugula salad dressed with a splash of olive oil, the juice of half a lemon, and a sprinkle of salt. Note: If you don't have an iron skillet, divide the batter between a pair of well-greased 9-inch pie pans.

SERVES 2 TO 4

3 tablespoons unsalted butter

4 extra-large eggs

½ cup whole milk

½ cup all-purpose white flour

½ cup grated Gruyère cheese

¼ cup chopped ham (3 to 4 thin slices)

2 to 3 sprigs parsley, finely chopped, for garnish

Lemon wedges, for garnish

Salt and freshly ground pepper, to taste

Preheat the oven to 425°F.

On the stove, melt the butter in a cast-iron skillet over low heat and make sure to run it up along the sides so that the entire pan is well greased.

In a blender, briefly pulse eggs, milk, and flour together—about 5 to 6 seconds total. Pour the batter into the skillet and top with cheese and ham. Bake 20 minutes, or until the top has puffed up and turned golden.

Garnish with parsley and a squeeze of lemon. Cut into wedges, and serve immediately.

Tip: For a sweet version of this recipe, omit the cheese and ham, and top the baked pancake with fresh berries, a light dusting of confectioners' sugar, and whipped cream.

Greta Garbo brought the drama as Grusinskaya, complete with entourage.

FEMALE <small>(1933)</small>

Menu
A SEDUCTIVE EVENING

Vodka Tonic

Boozy Olives

Bowtie Pasta with Spicy Vodka
Cream Sauce

N A CLASSIC REVERSAL OF GENDER ROLES, glamorous Ruth Chatterton plays Miss (Alison) Drake, a tireless business executive who turns office culture upside down by behaving in a most "unladylike" fashion. She employs male secretaries, pooh-poohs marriage, thrives on caffeine and board meetings, and appears to run the world from a giant office poised against the smokestacks of her family's automobile empire. She's also a master seductress who cherry-picks the handsomest men of her company and invites them home for pool parties and lavish suppers. When she's ready to make a sexual advance, she simply presses a secret button and a decanter of vodka appears on a tray. Think James Bond, but this one has curves.

To our modern mind-set, the feminist Miss Drake might seem out of place in the 1930s, and yet her character is one example among many strong female leads who ruffled feathers in pre-code cinema—challenging traditional values and bucking gender norms (try watching *Baby Face*). Eventually, her powers flicker and fizzle, and she is forced to surrender her independence (bummer!) when she meets her match. In Miss Drake's case, that's Jim Thorne, played by George Brent, who was Chatterton's actual husband at the time. One of the great actresses of the era, Chatterton brims with energy and elegant fashion here, making *Female* a riveting film to watch. It's also positively loaded with beverages, mostly vodka but also copious amounts of coffee.

Opposite: **Chatterton and a young lover, played by Phillip Reed**

"Cream and two sugars? My, you're a reckless woman!" —MISS DRAKE

While You're Watching...

★ The exterior shots of Miss Drake's mansion were filmed at Ennis House, designed by Frank Lloyd Wright.

★ Co-stars Ruth Chatterton and George Brent were married briefly, from 1932 to 1934.

Above: **Ruth Chatterton as Alison Drake, on the phone in bed, already conducting business**

Vodka Tonic

Female hit theaters in 1933, the same year Prohibition was repealed. The first vodka would have appeared in liquor stores and bars around the same time—brought to the United States by Ukrainian immigrant Rudolph Kunett, who befriended the Smirnoffs in Europe and acquired the rights to sell their family label. Prior to Prohibition, Americans drank gin, rum, and whiskey, so the prominent placement of vodka in this film would have been a coup—a novelty to moviegoers. In the film, Miss Drake drinks her vodka neat, in a long-stemmed sherry glass.

2 ounces vodka

4 ounces tonic water

Lime or lemon wedge, for garnish

Fill a rocks glass or collins glass with ice. Add vodka and top with tonic water. Garnish with a citrus wedge on the edge of the glass.

SEASONAL VODKA SODAS: *If you prefer soda to tonic, add interest with a few drops of bitters and a splash of in-season fruit juice. You can also muddle berries or cucumber slices in the bottom of the glass, along with fresh herbs. Try sage leaves and blackberries, basil and strawberries, or rosemary and blood orange. If you're having a party, make an infused vodka by adding 2 cups of washed, chopped fruit to 2 to 3 cups vodka. Store it out of the sunlight, and give it a good shake (and a quick taste!) every day until you get the desired flavor, usually 3 to 5 days. Then, strain well and refrigerate.*

Set the Scene ◄◄◄◄◄◄

This luxurious menu for two only needs one thing: throw pillows. You'll see why when you watch the movie. Set a low vase full of carnations on the coffee table and hunt for some crackly sounding organ music to play while you set about fixing drinks. After all, Miss Drake hired a private organist to play for all the intimate soirees held in her palatial home. Then, dim the lights, recline, and dine. After dinner, offer more vodka and—like the character—massages for dessert.

Boozy Olives

These make great martini olives, and they're delicious alongside cured meats—serve a dish of these with a rustic salami or some prosciutto rolled into thin cigarettes. This recipe is a culmination of research in curing olives as quickly as possible while at the same time preserving the integrity of good gin. It identifies and solves a couple of problems with existing methods. For example, some recipes have you heating the olives in the cure; this essentially bakes off the gin and results in a muted flavor. Why use good gin and then cook it?! Other recipes have you curing olives with olive oil in the marinade. But marinating with oil locks in flavor around the olive. How does the gin get in?!

Instead, this recipe reduces cure time and maximizes flavor by heating the olives and citrus, then adding them to unheated gin afterwards. The result is a fast, thorough infusion with bright, fresh gin notes in the olives. They're so wonderfully gin-y you may want to tone them down with a dash of olive oil before serving. Best of all, they're ready in about an hour.

SERVES 6 TO 8

1 jar (7½ ounces) Castelvetrano olives (retain the jar)

1 teaspoon lemon zest

4 ounces gin

2 to 3 tablespoons extra-virgin olive oil, for drizzling

Chatterton on a chaise lounge in her boudoir

Preheat the oven to 350°F.

Strain olives and reserve the brine for dirty Martinis and Bloody Marys. Place the olives in an oven-safe pan, such as a cast-iron skillet. Sprinkle with lemon zest.

Bake olives until thoroughly warmed, about 15 minutes. If the lemon zest is browning, the olives are done.

Return olives to their jar, top with gin, and replace the lid. Turn the jar gently to coat all the olives, and leave the mixture on the countertop for a half hour or more for the flavors to meld. If you're not going to use the olives immediately, store them in the refrigerator after a couple of hours of soaking.

To serve, strain the olives into a dish. Drizzle olive oil over them.

Bowtie Pasta with Spicy Vodka Cream Sauce

(PHOTO ON PAGES 32–33)

This simple sauce is sweet on the front end with a spicy kick on the finish. We like to serve it over bowtie pasta because, well, this movie is loaded with tuxedos and formalwear. Topped with fresh basil, this dish makes a quick but impressive weeknight meal. You can make it even more luxurious by adding shrimp or lump crabmeat. Just be clear about one thing: The vodka needs to cook off a bit here, otherwise the dish will taste bitter. A good 7-minute simmer before you add the cream will do the trick. Note: This recipe is easily doubled or tripled; we kept it small for intimate occasions.

SERVES 2

1 jar (12 ounces) roasted red peppers in olive oil, drained

1 small clove garlic

2 tablespoons tomato paste

½ teaspoon red pepper flakes

¼ cup vodka

½ pound bowtie pasta

¼ cup heavy cream

1 sprig fresh basil, leaves sliced into ribbons, for garnish

Freshly ground black pepper, for garnish

Puree the peppers and garlic in a blender until smooth, then pour the mixture into a saucepan over medium heat and add the tomato paste, pepper flakes, and vodka. Stir. In a separate pan, start cooking your pasta, according to the box instructions.

Simmer the vodka sauce for 7 to 8 minutes, or until the vodka has mostly cooked off and the sauce tastes sweet-hot, without being too bitter. (If it still tastes bitter, cook it a few minutes more or add a teaspoon or two of sugar. The cream will also mellow it.)

Add the cream to the sauce and stir. Heat gently. Drain pasta and separate into warmed bowls. Ladle sauce over the pasta and top with fresh basil and black pepper.

THE THIN MAN (1934)

Menu
MURDER MYSTERY DINNER

Marguerite (Dry Martini)

Whitefish Toasts

Rosemary Roasted Almonds

Oysters on the Half Shell

Box of Chocolates (suggested)

WITH COCKTAILS AT EVERY TURN, this toast to the end of Prohibition may be the ultimate drinking movie of the 1930s, and it's certainly one of the classiest—full of gilded hotel bars, booze-infused parlor gatherings, and sexy little nightcaps. This hard-drinking, high-class comedy based on the novel by Dashiell Hammett stars William Powell and Myrna Loy as husband-and-wife detective team Nick and Nora Charles. Their onscreen chemistry enchanted Depression-era moviegoers and percolated through an entire series, six films in all.

The success of *The Thin Man* was a shock for MGM—it was a B movie shot over just a couple of weeks. But critics and audiences loved it, and the film garnered multiple award nominations, including one for Best Picture at the Oscars. Today, it's credited with helping to set the tone for screwball comedy as a genre, thanks in part to the rollicking dialogue written by Albert Hackett and Frances Goodrich, themselves a husband-and-wife team. It's also one of few films from the period where characters truly revel in marital bliss. Nick and Nora relish every moment of their life together, even when they're just out for a walk with their dog, Asta. (Note the visual joke of that particular scene!)

Lighthearted and full of laughter, the Charleses make great company for a spirited anniversary party or a glamorous holiday-themed viewing. Set out some salty snacks and stir those martinis.

Opposite: **Myrna Loy and William Powell as Nick and Nora**

Set the Scene ◄◄◄◄◄◄

The Thin Man is a great excuse to host a glamorous cocktail party. Break out your silver and crystal serving trays, and ask your guests to dress up, if you wish. Tuxedos and evening gowns are de rigueur in *The Thin Man*, although Nick and Nora also bask in bathrobes—another choice, if you want to spin this as a fashionable pajama party. What's better than tipping back martinis and slurping oysters while wearing silky jimjams?

Above: William Powell, Myrna Loy, and Henry Wadsworth | *Opposite:* Asta

While You're Watching...

★ Asta, the little dog belonging to Nick and Nora, created nationwide zeal for wire fox terriers, a breed that was relatively unknown to American audiences at the time of the film.

★ The Charles' fabulous couture was designed by Dolly Tree, who designed costumes for the British stage before working in Hollywood. She created the look for rising stars, including Mae West, Jean Harlow, and Judy Garland.

★ Woody Allen used Nick and Nora as inspiration for his lead couple, the Liptons, in *Manhattan Murder Mystery* (1993).

"Now a Manhattan you shake to fox trot time, a Bronx to two-step time, a dry Martini you always shake to waltz time."

—NICK CHARLES

Marguerite (Dry Martini)

Nick Charles makes his grand first appearance onscreen teaching a bartender how to mix a proper martini. Keep in mind that in the 1930s, martinis were served with a higher percentage of vermouth than gin and usually in smaller doses. The recipe dates back to the 1880s and it originally called for gin, never vodka, along with orange bitters. Vodka martinis didn't come into vogue until James Bond came along in Dr. No (page 172). Other popular 1930s-era cocktails include the Manhattan (page 145) and the Bronx, both mentioned in film. They're all wonderful drinks, but intensely "spirituous," as we say now, so do pace yourself. And remember that a martini is stirred, not shaken.

2 ounces London dry gin

1 ounce dry vermouth

1 dash orange bitters

Lemon peel, for garnish

Stir ingredients with ice and strain into a chilled coupe glass. To garnish, twist the peel over the surface of the cocktail to express the oil then drop the peel into the drink.

Nora and Nick prepare to entertain

How to Batch a Pitcher of Cocktails

It's a snap to batch martinis in a pitcher, making 8 servings. Simply convert the ounces to cups in the recipe—2 cups of gin, 1 cup of vermouth, plus 8 dashes of orange bitters. You can apply this easy batching method to any drink recipe.

Whitefish Toasts (PHOTO ON PAGE 40)

After Prohibition, cocktail parties dominated the social scene, and yet there was a dilemma. "Now that everyone may drink with a clear conscience, many hostesses are wondering what to serve with the various beverages," observed Susan Mills in the Washington Post. *She noted that canapés featuring anchovies or other fish would be most appropriate, along with dainty sandwiches—hence our desire to return whitefish salad to the cocktail party circuit. Although you can purchase whitefish salad from delis, we like to take the mayo into our own hands and make whitefish salad from scratch. The result is fairly dry and won't make your toasts soggy. Arrange these on a tray and top them with a variety of eye-catching garnishes: capers, dill sprigs, walnut halves, hard-cooked quail egg halves, minced red pepper, or even a touch of trout roe. Note: Whitefish is a category of fish; we typically use whole smoked whiting from a seafood market.*

SERVES 6

For the whitefish salad

1 pound smoked whitefish (e.g., whiting), skinned, bones removed

3 green onions, minced (green and white parts)

1 celery rib, minced

1 tablespoon chopped fresh dill

⅓ cup mayonnaise

¼ cup sour cream

1 tablespoon fresh lemon juice

Freshly ground black pepper, to taste

For the toasts

1 box petit toasts or toasted pumpernickel rounds

1 English cucumber, thinly sliced into coins

Crumble the fish into a medium-size bowl or use a food processor to achieve a rough-chop. Add remaining salad ingredients and stir. Serve immediately or chill for up to a day.

For the toasts, place a slice of cucumber onto a round and top with a small spoonful of whitefish salad. Garnish as desired.

Tip: For additional munching, set out some assorted pickles and veg. We like to fill in around the edges with pickled beets, cornichons, and sliced radishes.

Rosemary Roasted Almonds

The smell of these almonds warms the house. We like to pop them into the oven just before guests arrive. Try using roasted, unsalted almonds here—they maintain better crunch than starting with raw almonds.

SERVES 6

2 cups almonds

1 tablespoon extra-virgin olive oil

1 teaspoon smoked paprika

1 tablespoon chopped fresh rosemary

½ teaspoon sea salt

Preheat the oven to 325°F and line a cookie sheet with tinfoil or parchment paper. (A cast-iron skillet also works well—no need to line it.)

Toss the ingredients together in a medium-size bowl and stir. Then spread the almonds on a cookie sheet in a single layer. Roast for 18 to 20 minutes, or until lightly toasted. Cool and store in a jar on the counter; they are most flavorful on the day they are made.

Oysters on the Half Shell

Look for the freshest oysters you can find. Then, before guests arrive make sure you have an oyster knife and some kitchen rags on hand for shucking. If you're not an experienced shucker, pop onto the Internet for a demonstration. You'll also want to crush some ice in advance—easily done by filling a freezer bag with ice cubes and whapping them with a rolling pin. Shuck those babies and set them on a serving platter lined with crushed ice and lemon or lime wedges. Decadent!

CHAINED (1934)

Menu

FARM-TO-TABLE LUNCH

Sherry Flip

Roasted Chicken with Cider Gastrique

Radish Salad with Buttermilk Dressing

THE FIFTH COLLABORATION BETWEEN MEGASTARS Clark Gable and Joan Crawford, *Chained* is a hot and stylish tour de force—especially for Gable, who seems to come into his own in this role as a dashing tempter. From the moment you see the chic opening scene of Diane Lovering (Crawford) crossing the Hudson River in a speedboat—regally standing in a fashionable suit—you're transported to a world of glamour and charming banter.

    Chained is the story of shipping magnate Richard Field (Otto Kruger), who wants to marry his young mistress, Diane Lovering, but can't because his wife won't agree to a divorce. The consummate sugar daddy, Field sends Lovering on a cruise to Buenos Aires, intending to distract her from his complex marital woes. On the cruise, she meets dashing Mike Bradley (Gable), who wastes no time in winning Diane's affections. Although she tries to resist, she can't, especially after he whisks her off to his ranch in Argentina. Caught between two wealthy suitors, she is forced to choose one. Should she return to the staid older man who gave her everything, or run off with her luscious new lover?

    Two great food and drink scenes bookend Diane's alliance with Mike Bradley. One is on the ship when she is drinking Sherry Flips, which Mike considers much too dotty for her age; he encourages Diane instead to drink Daiquiris (page 99). The other is a huge spread on Mike's ranch, after which he and even Diane unbuckle their belts to sit back and digest—the inspiration for this menu! Get ready for a sumptuous script, wild fashion, and wonderful quips like "shut the door!" and "holy cats!"

Opposite: **Joan Crawford**

While You're Watching...

★ Crawford's biological father, Thomas Le Sueur, visited her on the set of *Chained*. It was the only time they ever met.

★ Crawford and Gable sizzle on screen together because the chemistry is real; much of the witty repartee in *Chained* is ad-libbed, and director Clarence Brown left it in.

Set the Scene ◄◄◄◄◄◄

Just like the meal in the movie, this is a simple farm repast after a hard day's work (or a romp in the fields). Set out a jug of milk, include a loaf of bread and butter, and focus on the purity of flavors in the recipes. Despite the casual atmosphere, the actors are ever-chic even when they're getting dirty, so don't hesitate to break out your suits and dresses or, better yet, riding clothes. You'll notice that Joan Crawford is never without exquisite attire and perfectly plucked eyebrows. Swoon.

Crawford and Gable on a cruise to Buenos Aires

"Sherry flip? They give that to people with stomach trouble and the gout. They serve it in old people's homes on Christmas."

—MIKE BRADLEY

Sherry Flip

This cocktail becomes the symbolic divide between Diane Lovering's old life—marked by the conventionality of the Sherry Flip (a rather heavy drink)—and the much faster world of Mike Bradley, represented by the modern and free-wheeling Daiquiri (page 99). We suggest starting the movie with this flip and ending it with a Daiquiri.

2 ounces sherry, preferably Oloroso

1 small fresh egg

½ ounce simple syrup (1:1 sugar and water)

Freshly grated nutmeg, for garnish

Shake sherry, egg, and simple syrup together without ice. Add ice, and shake again. Strain into a wine glass and garnish with nutmeg.

Radish Salad with Buttermilk Dressing

Creamy and flecked with herbs, this is one of our go-to dressings. If you have any left over, use it as dip for raw vegetables, or toss it with cold, chopped leftover chicken for a quick chicken salad.

2 heads Boston lettuce, leaves torn

6 radishes, sliced

1 green onion, sliced

1 medium shallot, thinly sliced

1 medium garlic clove, minced

1 cup buttermilk

½ cup mayonnaise

2 tablespoons lime juice (1 to 2 limes)

½ cup chopped fresh basil

½ cup chopped flat-leaf parsley

¼ teaspoon salt

In a medium bowl, combine lettuce, radish, and scallion. In a blender, combine remainder of the ingredients and blend until creamy. Pour over salad and toss.

Opposite: **A lovestruck Mike (Gable) and Diane (Crawford)**

Roasted Chicken with Cider Gastrique

The sweet-and-sour combination for the gastrique here promises one of the easiest and tastiest roasted chicken recipes we know. The simplicity of this dish is a perfect foil to the herbaceous buttermilk and herb dressing on the salad, making for a memorable meal.

SERVES 4

For the chicken

1 chicken (4 to 5 pounds)

4 tablespoons unsalted butter, softened

½ lemon

For the gastrique

½ cup rice vinegar

½ cup apple cider vinegar

½ cup honey

2 allspice berries, ground (about ¼ teaspoon)

½ star anise, ground (about ¼ teaspoon)

Preheat the oven to 425°F.

Rub the chicken with butter, being sure to get some under the skin on the breasts and thighs (use the end of a spoon to open the areas, if necessary). Place the lemon half in the cavity.

In a roasting pan, cook the chicken, breast-side up, for 30 minutes. While the chicken is cooking, make the gastrique (glaze) in a small saucepan by bringing the vinegars to a boil and then letting it simmer for 10 minutes. Add honey and spices and simmer for 5 more minutes.

Baste the chicken with the glaze, flipping it breast-side down, and cook for another 20 minutes. Baste and turn the chicken over again, breast-side up for about 20 minutes longer.

Remove the bird from the oven, and let rest for 10 minutes before carving.

DODSWORTH (1936)

WHO WANTS TO GROW OLD? Most definitely not Fran Dodsworth (Ruth Chatterton), a housewife and mother hell-bent on fleeing the Midwest and making up for lost time after her busy husband retires. But travel has a funny way of revealing character, and when Sam Dodsworth (Walter Huston) and Fran travel by steamship to Europe, they discover that they have less in common than they thought—but plenty in common with charming fellow passengers! Cue up some sultry jazz and pour yourself a stiff drink, or two—you'll need them to keep up with the Dodsworths as they make hay all the way across the Atlantic.

Based on a book by Sinclair Lewis, *Dodsworth* features a terrific script, phenomenal acting, great pacing, and a truly gripping look at ambitious dreamers who seek to reinvent themselves. The film also marked a breakthrough for gifted director William Wyler, who went on to direct *Roman Holiday* (page 119) and *Funny Girl* (page 189), among others. Though *Dodsworth* wasn't the box office success that producer Samuel Goldwyn hoped for, critics praised it and the film received an impressive seven Oscar nominations. Today, watching these characters struggle to relax feels eerily relevant. "I want a new life," Mr. Dodsworth exclaims after he tries to quit striving. "I'll enjoy life now even if it kills me, and it probably will."

Later, Fran's lover admonishes her, "I live in the present. Why don't you?"

Full of travel scenes set in Paris, London, and Naples, *Dodsworth* is a caper worthy of a transatlantic feast—break out your highball glasses, get some crusty baguettes, and invite your most interesting friends over for a classic Neapolitan seafood stew.

Opposite: **At Union Motors**

Set the Scene ◄◄◄◄◄◄

Dodsworth's most tender moments take place in Naples at the villa of Edith Cortright (Mary Astor), where Samuel Dodsworth begins to relax and enjoy life—fishing and flirting himself silly. Simplicity works best here, in accordance with Huston's and Astor's unfussy characters. Spread out a checkered tablecloth, light a single candle. Serve highballs as guests arrive, along with some light munchies that won't fill them up, like Boozy Olives (page 34) or Rosemary Roasted Almonds (page 143). Serve wine with the stew, followed by a round of espresso and biscotti.

Highball

Dodsworth is a straightforward man, and this is a straightforward drink. The choice is a highball, or specifically, Scotch and Soda, which he frequently orders in the movie or makes himself. Highballs are any combination of liquor and soda together, served in a tall glass with ice.

2 ounces Scotch

4 ounces soda water

In a tall (highball) glass, add a few ice cubes. Add Scotch, then soda, and serve.

While You're Watching...

★ During the making of this film, actress Mary Astor was in the middle of a nasty public divorce and custody battle. She claimed her role as Edith was her all-time favorite, and she credited it with helping keep her sanity.

★ Look for director William Wyler's cameo as a violin player during the scene at a Vienna nightclub where Fran dances with her paramour, Kurt von Obersdorf (Gregory Gaye).

Opposite: **Walter Huston and Mary Astor** | *Above:* **Ruth Chatterton and Walter Huston**

Neapolitan Seafood Stew

This classic seafood stew is a snap to prepare as long as you have everything prepped in advance—it's more assembly and timing than anything. Have the bread toasted and guests ready as you enter the final phase of cooking the seafood. And don't be afraid to poke a piece of fish to check if it's done—this isn't fussy! Wine pairing note: Surprisingly, for a region so far south, the area around Naples makes excellent white wine—look for Campanian whites, like Greco di Tufo or Fiano. Short of this, a dry white will work well.

SERVES 6 TO 8

3 tablespoons extra-virgin olive oil

4 garlic cloves, squashed and sliced thin

1 teaspoon red pepper flakes

3 celery ribs, chopped

2 medium yellow onions, diced

2 plum tomatoes, diced

1 bunch parsley, finely chopped

1½ cups dry white wine

2 to 3 pounds mixed fish

2 cups (16 ounces) seafood stock, divided

1 pound fresh clams

2 pounds fresh mussels

Salt and freshly ground black pepper, to taste

"I want to sit under a linden tree with nothing more important to worry about . . . than the temperature of the beer." —SAM DODSWORTH

In a large soup pot or saucepan, sweat the garlic cloves in oil on medium-high heat until fragrant, about 3 minutes. (Do not let the garlic brown, or it will taste bitter.)

Add red pepper flakes, celery, and onions, and cook until the onions are translucent but not browned, about 3 to 5 minutes. Add the tomatoes and parsley. Once the tomatoes release their juices, after about 5 more minutes, add the wine.

Bring the mixture to a simmer, then toss in the fish and add as much seafood stock as necessary to submerge. Cook for 5 minutes, or until the fish is flaky. (This will depend on the size of your pieces.)

Add the clams and mussels, then the remainder of the stock and cook over medium heat with the lid on until the clams and mussels steam open, about 5 to 10 minutes. Add salt and pepper to taste.

Serve in shallow bowls with toasted bread.

STAGECOACH (1939)

Menu

A CHUCKWAGON SUPPER

Duke's Bourbon Paloma

Bourbon Chili

Spicy Popcorn

IRECTOR JOHN FORD'S FIRST SOUND WESTERN CAPTURES LIFE along a dusty stagecoach route with a gripping cast of characters. The star, John Wayne, plays the Ringo Kid—a good-bad dreamboat bent on revenge, who rises from the stunning desert landscape of Utah's Monument Valley with a saddle over one arm. The role launched Wayne's career.

As the coach rides through dangerous Apache territory, the passengers from various social strata reveal their true stories, from whiskey salesman Samuel Peacock (Donald Meek) to Confederate gambler Hatfield (John Carradine), to the pregnant Mrs. Mallory (Louise Platt). Along the way, Ringo drawls his way into a salty love affair with one of the ladies on board and manages to protect the clumsy coach from toppling into enemy hands—all while maintaining his characteristic smooth-man act.

Nominated for seven Academy Awards (it won for Best Scoring and Best Supporting Actor), *Stagecoach* is both a well-paced action and adventure film, as well as a meaningful story of redemption—with Hollywood's most alluring cowboy at the helm. Let the rough-hewn desert landscape and Wayne's brooding close-ups sweep you away, as you sip his namesake cocktail.

Opposite: **Claire Trevor and John Wayne**

Duke's Bourbon Paloma

Wayne loved tequila and was one of the first American stars to embrace the liquor from across the border. But he also loved whiskey and was known to carry a box of bottles with him so he could make his own blends. His blend is re-created today in Duke Bourbon, with involvement from son Ethan Wayne. In this cocktail, the popular tequila-based Paloma gets a makeover with a Kentucky twist. Sweet bourbon loves grapefruit, and this simple twist on a classic is not only refreshing but an ideal pairing with chili or other spicy foods.

2 ounces bourbon

2 ounces fresh grapefruit juice

½ ounce fresh lime juice

Shake ingredients with ice and pour into a rocks glass, ice and all.

Spicy Popcorn

It takes almost no additional work to take traditional movie night popcorn to new heights with a few powders that most kitchens have on hand. Spicy with a citrus lift, this popcorn is the perfect foil for a western. Note: Have a large paper bag ready for tossing the popcorn when it comes off the stove.

½ cup popcorn kernels

3 tablespoons vegetable oil

1 teaspoon sea salt

1 teaspoon chili powder

½ teaspoon garlic salt

¼ teaspoon ground cumin

¼ teaspoon smoked paprika

Lime zest, for garnish

In a half-cup measuring cup, measure out the popcorn and pour oil into the cup to fill it (about 3 tablespoons). This will coat the kernels. Heat a medium-size stockpot or Dutch oven, add popcorn and oil, and cover with a lid. Cook 2 to 3 minutes, or until popcorn nearly stops popping.

Remove the popcorn from the heat and dump it into a paper bag, then add salt, chili powder, garlic salt, cumin, and paprika. Toss thoroughly and serve in bowls with grated lime zest.

"Well, there are some things a man just can't run away from."

—THE RINGO KID

Bourbon Chili

Make no mistake, this is competition chili. Toasting the ancho chiles first ensures a depth of flavor that rings simple and true—there's no chili powder or fake smoke here, just straight-shooting Tex-Mex ingredients that will ensure your legendary status among guests. While the chili can be topped with anything you please (and we like to put out a garnish spread including everything from corn chips to fresh cilantro), we find that radishes and orange zest bring out the most bourbon-happy flavors. Here's to life on the rugged open road!

SERVES 6 TO 8

5 or 6 dried ancho chiles (4 ounces)

2 tablespoons ground cumin

2 tablespoons ground coriander

1 tablespoon freshly ground black pepper

2 tablespoons all-purpose white flour

1 pound pork shoulder, cut into ½-inch cubes

1 pound chuck roast, cut into ½-inch cubes

6 garlic cloves, unpeeled

3 tablespoons vegetable oil

2 medium onions, chopped

1 red bell pepper, chopped

1 hot banana pepper, chopped

2 tablespoons paprika

2 teaspoons Mexican oregano

1 bay leaf

1 can (15 ounces) diced tomatoes

¼ cup apple cider vinegar

3½ cups beef stock, divided

1 tablespoon molasses

1 can (15 ounces) kidney beans, drained and rinsed

½ cup bourbon

Salt, to taste

Radishes, chopped or minced, for garnish

Crème fraîche (or plain yogurt), for garnish

Orange zest, for garnish

Break off chile stems, open chiles, and discard the seeds. Open the chiles flat and toast them, skin-side up, in a skillet on medium-high heat for just a few seconds, until they brown but not blacken. Flip chiles and cook the other side. Hold them down with a spatula and work in batches, if needed. Remove the chiles from the skillet to a bowl, add enough warm water until the chiles are submerged, then cover the bowl, and let them rehydrate for 30 minutes.

Combine cumin, coriander, black pepper, and flour in a medium mixing bowl. Toss the pork and beef in spices and set

aside. In an ungreased skillet on medium heat, roast the garlic cloves until browned and soft to the touch (they may blacken slightly)—about 15 minutes. Remove garlic from the pan, then let cool and slip off the skins. Set aside.

In a large pot over medium-high heat, fry the beef and the pork in the oil until browned, working in batches if necessary. Remove from the pan and set aside. Add onions to the pot and lightly brown them, about 4 minutes, then add red pepper and banana pepper, paprika, oregano, bay leaf, tomatoes, and vinegar.

Drain the chiles, and put them in a blender or food processor with the garlic. Add 1½ cups beef stock slowly to make a smooth puree. Using a spatula to work it through, strain the puree through a mesh strainer, discarding the solids. Add the strained puree to the pot. Add remaining stock and molasses. Simmer the chili partially covered for 30 minutes.

Add kidney beans and cook another 30 minutes. Douse with bourbon, stir briefly, and add salt to taste. Serve in bowls garnished with radish, crème fraîche, and orange zest.

Above: **The stagecoach**

Set the Scene ◄◄◄◄◄

Strap on your spurs and dust off your cowboy hats. If you can, stage a chuckwagon supper with metal plates, big wooden spoons, and a cast-iron pot. Throw your guests checkered dish towels for napkins. We like to have a bottle of both tequila and bourbon handy, so we can make Palomas both ways. But there's no reason to stop there. This movie is an excellent excuse for a chili cook-off (which this recipe is sure to win!), a bourbon tasting, or whatever friendly competitive hijinks you'd like to get up to. Just don't tell the sheriff.

While You're Watching...

★ The hat John Wayne wears in *Stagecoach* was his own. He wore it in Westerns for the next couple of decades.

★ When it was first released, the film was called "the *Grand Hotel* on wheels"—a reference to the 1932 film, which also featured an ensemble of strong characters with intertwining storylines.

★ John Wayne was nicknamed "The Duke" as a child. He had a dog named Duke, and people started referring to Wayne as "Little Duke." His real name was Marion Mitchell Morrison.

The ensemble cast of characters at the dinner table

THE PHILADELPHIA STORY (1940)

Menu

LUNCH ON THE MAIN LINE

Stinger

Upscale Cheesesteak with Truffle Brie

Mints or Chocolates (suggested)

B Y THE TIME KATHARINE HEPBURN APPEARED IN *THE PHILADELPHIA Story*, she was already a star, but she was perceived as "box office poison" after several commercial flops. *The Philadelphia Story* signaled her resurrection. Here she plays Tracy Lord, a swan-like socialite who survives a sticky divorce and embarks upon a new engagement. When a pair of tabloid journalists descend—and scheme to finagle their way into the wedding party—Tracy and her family play along to cover up a family scandal. That's how she meets newspaper writer Macaulay Connor (James Stewart). Their initial disdain for one another turns to cheeky banter, then mutual infatuation. After all, Tracy loves words, too—the film opens with her spelling out "omelet" for a crossword.

Loaded with opulent scenes of the Lord family's Main Line mansion, including its glamorous pool house, *The Philadelphia Story* is a romantic comedy filled with fine taste and electrifying friction. Hepburn's character was written for her, and her wit snaps and

Opposite: **Katharine Hepburn and James Stewart toasting with cocktails in the garden**

sparks like a bonfire, especially when its flames are fed by the men in her midst, including Cary Grant (who plays her on-the-wagon ex-husband) and John Howard (who plays her pretentious fiancé, George Kittredge).

This film opened the day after Christmas in 1940 and generated so much buzz that it drew the longest line Radio City Music Hall had ever seen. It's a treat to watch any time of year, especially with a Champagne bucket within reach.

Set the Scene ◀◀◀◀◀

The set of this film is rich with formal table settings, though our meal is casual—based upon the classic Philadelphia working man's sandwich. We like to start a *Philadelphia Story* movie party by offering guests Champagne or martinis with olives—Tracy's father (John Halliday) fixes them in the movie as she steps out of the pool. Since the Stinger appears late in the film, we like to serve a round after the cheesesteak—as dessert, alongside dark chocolate. Got a model sailboat or some vintage cameras lying around? Work them into a centerpiece, along with leather-bound books, silver trophies, equestrian-themed baubles, and ivy.

While You're Watching ...

★ Katharine Hepburn in trousers was trailblazing. In the early 1940s, it was unusual for women to wear pants in public. Hepburn insisted on wearing them in the opening scene, in spite of director George Cukor's objections, and she continued to wear them—in many styles—throughout the film.

★ If you enjoy Hepburn's acid tongue here, try watching *Adam's Rib* (page 96).

Right: **Tracy (Hepburn) and Dinah Lord (Virginia Weidler)** | *Opposite:* **Day drinking on the Main Line**

Stinger

Mint and brandy? Try asking an old country club bartender to fix you one—he'll remember when this was the after-dinner drink of choice for the fast crowd. Pairing these two ingredients can be traced back to 1892 (when it was called the Judge), but it resurfaced in the 1940s, when brandy was fashionable. Note that bartenders often shake this drink to give it a nice froth. It can also be made with gin instead of brandy. In the movie, Uncle Willy refers to this recipe as a formula "that's said to pop the pennies off dead Irishmen."

2 ounces brandy

1 ounce white crème de menthe (or Death's Door Wondermint)

Sprig of mint, for garnish

Shake ingredients with ice and strain into a brandy snifter or rocks glass filled with crushed ice. Garnish with mint.

Upscale Cheesesteak with Truffle Brie

This twist on a classic is quick and luscious, and the recipe scales up or down easily. If you want to create a build-your-own cheesesteak bar, keep the onions and peppers separate and offer a buffet of toppings: provolone, pickled peppers, sautéed mushrooms. We like to serve this meal with a relish tray arranged in a crystal dish, along with a bowl of kettle chips. Wine pairing note: Chardonnay is great with black truffles, or, if you prefer red, try a Barbaresco.

SERVES 4

1½ pounds rib eye steak

2 tablespoons extra-virgin olive oil

1 medium yellow onion, halved and thinly sliced

½ green bell pepper, seeded and thinly sliced (optional)

2 large garlic cloves, minced

1 teaspoon salt

½ teaspoon freshly ground black pepper

4 crusty rolls

½ pound Truffle Brie, room temperature (we like Marin French)

2 tablespoons chopped fresh chives

"Whiskey is a slap on the back, and Champagne's heavy mist before my eyes."

—MACAULAY CONNOR

Slice the steak thinly—it helps to work with frozen meat, so thaw it slightly if it's been in the freezer, or freeze it for about 45 minutes if it's fresh. Using a sharp knife, cut it against the grain into thin slices. Set aside.

Preheat a large skillet over medium heat. Add the olive oil and sauté the onions for 5 minutes, or until translucent. Then add peppers and sauté until soft, about another 5 minutes. Slide these onto a plate and set aside.

Drop the garlic into the hot skillet, followed by meat and seasoning. Cook for about 10 minutes over medium heat, or just until the pink disappears. Do not overcook the meat, or it will become tough. When it's finished, fold the onions and peppers back into the mixture and remove the skillet from the heat.

To serve, slather the rolls with Truffle Brie, and top with the hot steak mixture so that the cheese melts. Garnish with chives.

CASABLANCA (1942)

Menu

A MOROCCAN FAREWELL

French 75

Roasted Eggplant Tagine

OH, *CASABLANCA!* This romantic melodrama appears on more best-of lists than just about any other film of its era. Universally beloved for its exotic set and compelling characters, *Casablanca* opens at Rick's Café Américain, a glittering nightclub filled with expats stuck in French colonial Morocco at the dawn of World War II. Rick Blaine (Humphrey Bogart) serves as the white-tuxedoed host who keeps one eye on the gambling tables and another on the door, watching for Nazis. A piano trills merrily along, until an old flame appears (Ingrid Bergman), shaking Rick's stoic presence.

Nominated for eight Academy Awards, *Casablanca* is both a Hollywood fairy tale and a relic of wartime propaganda—making the French 75, named after a military cannon, a well-matched drink. It appears briefly in the film and is a perfect match for the bubbling emotions and bright energy of the film's stars. Supporting actors Peter Lorre (the smarmy smuggler, Ugarte), Dooley Wilson (the club's piano player, Sam), and Claude Rains (the French official, Louis Renault) also deliver stellar performances.

Starring an aromatic tagine—a traditional Moroccan dish—this menu serves as a lovely backdrop to a movie that is subtly heroic and seriously passionate. Break out your fezzes and fedoras.

Opposite: **Humphrey Bogart and Ingrid Bergman as Rick and Ilsa**

French 75

This drink hails from Harry's New York bar in Paris around 1915 and gets its name from a French cannon that helped win World War I; returning pilots popularized it stateside. Elegant and zesty, this can be served either straight up in a coupe or on the rocks in a highball glass with a lemon wheel.

1 ounce gin

½ ounce fresh lemon juice

½ ounce simple syrup (1:1 sugar and water)

4 ounces Champagne (or Crémant)

Lemon peel, for garnish

Shake the gin, lemon juice, and syrup together on ice. Strain over ice into a chilled highball glass. Top off with Champagne. To garnish, run the lemon peel around the rim of the glass, then drop it into the drink.

Above: **Humphrey Bogart and Ingrid Bergman** | *Opposite:* **Dooley Wilson and Humphrey Bogart**

"Of all the gin joints in all the towns in all the world, she walks into mine." —RICK

Roasted Eggplant Tagine

Simplicity itself, this delightful tagine brings the flavors of North Africa to your kitchen without any fuss. If you can find the spice mix ras el hanout at a local store (it's also readily available online), it makes this recipe quicker. If not, the DIY version below is easy. You may even want to make a double or triple batch of this mixture so you can use it again for a rub or to make another Moroccan dish. It's a glorious flavor combination.

SERVES 2 TO 4

For the tagine

1½ cups chicken stock, divided

1 tablespoon unsalted butter

¾ cup pearl couscous

3 teaspoons extra-virgin olive oil

4 cloves garlic, minced

½ teaspoon salt

2 teaspoons ras el hanout (see below)

1 can (15 ounces) diced tomatoes

2 small eggplants, diced (about 4 cups)

1 can (15 ounces) chickpeas, drained

4 Medjool dates, pitted and chopped

3 tablespoons almonds, roughly chopped and toasted, for garnish

1 small bunch mint, chopped, for garnish

Plain yogurt, for garnish

For the ras el hanout

¼ teaspoon ground ginger

¼ teaspoon ground coriander

¼ teaspoon ground turmeric

¼ teaspoon ground nutmeg

¼ teaspoon ground allspice

¼ teaspoon paprika

¼ teaspoon ground cloves

¼ teaspoon freshly ground black pepper

In a saucepan, boil 1 cup chicken stock with butter. Add couscous, stir, then remove from heat and cover.

Heat oil in a saucepan over medium-high heat. Add the garlic, salt, and spices and cook until garlic is translucent and the spices are lightly toasted, about 3 minutes.

Add tomatoes, eggplant, chickpeas, dates, and ½ cup of chicken stock. Bring to a boil, cover, and then simmer on medium, stirring occasionally, for 10 to 15 minutes or until eggplant has softened.

To serve, set out shallow bowls. Fluff the couscous and divide it among the bowls. Then, top with tagine and garnish with almonds, mint, and a scoop of yogurt.

Set the Scene ◄◄◄◄◄◄

Invoke Morocco with clay bowls, a blue-and-white tablecloth, and hanging lanterns. If you own a piano, invite at least one friend who can tickle the ivories. The architecture in this film is stunning, and so are its stars—who dress almost entirely in white. Plan a summer evening viewing party, and set off a few fireworks after the show. Or, serve another round of French 75s on the patio while replaying the movie's famous, misty-eye-making theme song, "As Time Goes By."

While You're Watching...

★ The character of Rick Blaine was Bogart's first role as a romantic hero (prior to this, he usually played gangsters or hard-boiled detectives). He and Bergman only shared the screen this once. She was taller than he was, which required him to sit on pillows when they shared a couch during their love scene.

★ *Casablanca* has many famous quotes, and even a well-known misquote: "Play it again, Sam." In fact, Bogart never utters those exact words. When he requests the film's iconic love song ("As Time Goes By"), he simply says "Play it" to Sam.

Right: **The crowd at Rick's is regaled by Sam's playing.**

THE LADY FROM SHANGHAI (1947)

"I told you...
you know
nothing
about
wickedness"

Rita Orson
HAYWORTH · WELLES
The LADY *from* SHANGHAI

Menu
ASIA MEETS THE MEXICAN RIVIERA

Margarita

Chicken Fried Rice and Green Apple Tacos

Sesame Guacamole with Jicama

THE OH-SO-GLAMOROUS RITA HAYWORTH LEAPED AT THE CHANCE to play Elsa Bannister in this grizzly whodunit, directed by Orson Welles (her second husband), who also stars in the film. Welles had made a name for himself with *Citizen Kane* (1941) and *The Magnificent Ambersons* (1942), and Hayworth was eager to take on a serious dramatic role under his direction. She also hoped the film might rekindle their marriage, since she and Welles were on the rocks. (It didn't.) You can read the pain in her eyes when the camera hovers above her as she sunbathes on yachts and beaches, playing the sexy young wife of decrepit millionaire Arthur Bannister (Everett Sloane).

Shot in Mexico and California, *The Lady from Shanghai* includes one of the most magical cocktail scenes—watch for the beach picnic about 20 minutes in, where cocktails are prepared hammock-side while Mr. and Mrs. Bannister lounge together, lit only by torches. Our fusion menu is inspired by this moment, and by references to Shanghai both early in the film and at the end, when Mrs. Bannister and her lover, Mike O'Hara (Welles), rendez-vous in the seats of a Chinese theatre.

Welles deliberately shot the film in a documentary style, which lends a lugubrious and noir-ish tone—perfect for sipping a salty drink and watching the slow unraveling of intricate plotlines.

Opposite: **The stylized publicity stills reflect the off-kilter tenor of *The Lady from Shanghai*.**

"Living on a hook takes away your appetite." —MIKE O'HARA

Margarita

The origins of the Margarita are much disputed. There's mention of a Tequila Daisy (Margarita means "daisy" in Spanish) as early as 1936, but no mention of a Margarita proper occurs until 1953 in Esquire *magazine. Some associate the drink with Rita Hayworth (born Margarita Cansino), the 1940s "love goddess." Still other historians believe the Margarita is an Anglo-British invention derived from the Sidecar or the Picador cocktail. Whatever its origin, it pairs perfectly here with guac and tacos.*

2 ounces blanco tequila

1 ounce triple sec

1 ounce fresh lime juice

Sea salt, to rim the glass (optional)

Lime wedge, for garnish

To rim a rocks glass with salt, run a wedge of lime around the lip to wet it, then dunk the glass into a saucer of salt. Then, fill the glass with ice. Shake tequila, triple sec, and lime juice with ice. Strain into the prepared glass. Garnish with lime.

Femme fatale Rita Hayworth in a broken mirror

Chicken Fried Rice and Green Apple Tacos

Sure, you can order fried rice for take-out. But it is infinitely better made at home, and this quick dish is a true crowd pleaser. Strange as it might sound, this recipe combines the best of two worlds—the tartness and crunch of the green apples work magnificently to bring together Asian-based flavors with those of the Americas.

SERVES 6 TO 8

4 large eggs

2 tablespoons sesame oil

3 tablespoons unsalted butter

1 medium onion, chopped

3 cloves garlic, minced

4 cups rice, cooked

1 pound chicken breast, cooked and cut into half-inch cubes

1 bag (10 ounces) frozen peas and carrots, thawed

¼ cup soy sauce

Flour or corn tortilla shells

2 green apples, cored and thinly sliced

Hot sauce, preferably El Yucateco Jalapeño

In a small bowl, whisk the eggs and set aside. In a large skillet or wok, heat oil and butter on medium-high heat. Add the onion and cook until translucent, about 4 minutes. Then add garlic and stir briefly.

Add cooked rice and chicken, and cook until mixture crisps slightly on the bottom of the pan, about 5 minutes. Add peas and carrots. Cook and stir for another 5 minutes.

Make a reservoir in the rice by sweeping it against the sides of your pan, and pour in the whisked eggs, stirring them with a spoon until they scramble. When they're cooked, mix everything in the pan together, while adding the soy sauce.

Serve fried rice in soft tortillas or hard shells with slices of green apple in the tacos. Garnish with hot sauce.

Sesame Guacamole with Jicama

(PHOTO ON PAGE 82)

Jicama adds delightful crisp texture while the toasted sesame contributes an earthy nuttiness to this Asian-Mexican fusion guacamole. Easy to prepare and wildly addictive, you may never make traditional guac again!

3 ripe avocados, halved and pitted

1 small red onion, finely chopped or grated

½ cup peeled and finely diced jicama

2 tablespoons chopped cilantro

1 jalapeño, seeded and finely chopped

1½ tablespoons lime juice

½ teaspoon toasted sesame oil

1 teaspoon freshly ground black pepper

1 teaspoon salt

1 green onion, chopped, for garnish

1 teaspoon toasted sesame seeds, for garnish

Warm tortilla chips, for serving

In a medium bowl, mash avocados with a fork or potato masher. Stir in onion, jicama, cilantro, jalapeño, lime juice, sesame oil, pepper, and salt. Garnish with green onions and sesame seeds. Serve with warm tortilla chips.

Orson Welles and Rita Hayworth

Orson Welles, as Michael O'Hara, in a hall of mirrors

Set the Scene ◄◄◄◄◄◄

Channel this film's Mexican flavor and its Pacific connection with this menu and its table setting—think sea grass placemats, baskets of citrus, and colorful flowers. Black-and-white polka dots, as seen on Hayworth's dress and later on an ascot, can be a fun accent to carry over with napkins or ribbon. Keep the lights low and set out plenty of candles. If you want to serve dessert, offer ice cream bars (you'll see one early in the film).

While You're Watching...

★ Actor Errol Flynn was the owner of the yacht *Zaca*, on which much of the movie takes place. It can be seen in the background in a scene outside the cantina.

★ Look for the scene where Orson Welles runs past a movie poster for *Resurrection* (1927). The movie starred Dolores del Rio, his former girlfriend.

★ Welles asked Hayworth to change her hair from signature long red locks to a short blonde style for the role of Elsa. The transformation became part of a publicity stunt, billed as "The Million Dollar Haircut," with hordes of Hollywood photographers on site to chronicle Hayworth's falling tresses. Columbia studio head Harry Cohn was horrified; Welles hadn't consulted him about the cut, and Cohn hated the new look.

THE LADY FROM SHANGHAI (1947) **87**

ROPE (1948)

Menu

A MURDER AND CANAPÉ

Art of Choke

Camembert in a Coffin

Parmigiano Rope Twists

ALFRED HITCHCOCK'S GHOULISHLY PLAYFUL *ROPE* OPENS WITH A murder: Two prep school chums strangle a mutual friend to prove a point, then host a cocktail party over his dead body. As a cruel joke, they stow their victim in a wooden trunk and refashion it as a buffet table. While guests nosh crudités and sip cocktails, no one suspects the macabre scene that took place just hours before the party—except one guest, the boys' former headmaster (James Stewart). Will the "perfect murder" be revealed and ruin the festivities?

Full of drinks and double entendre (about "farewell parties" and "strangling"), *Rope* is a natural pairing for a semiformal affair with a Champagne drinking game—a sip for every nefarious innuendo? Hitchcock's artistry gleams here, as does his love of style. Note how the film, based on a stage play, relies on long takes to create a seamless feel, as if the whole film was captured by a single camera in the hands of a creepy voyeur.

Prepare a feast, or a few nibbles, and serve it on a trunk, if you have one!

Above: **Director Alfred Hitchcock with the movie's namesake prop** | *Opposite:* **Rupert (James Stewart) pretending to open the chest**

"What is going on here?"
—PHILLIP

"A party but quite a
peculiar party."
—RUPERT

Art of Choke

This dark, slightly bitter drink, developed by Kyle Davidson at Chicago's Violet Hour cocktail bar, is Hitchcock ready. Cynar is an Italian digestif made from artichokes, hence the name "Art of Choke." Consider this a stomach soother if horror makes you tense.

2 small mint sprigs, divided

1 ounce light rum

1 ounce Cynar

¼ ounce green Chartreuse

⅛ ounce fresh lime juice

⅛ ounce rich Demerara syrup (2:1 Demerara sugar and warm water)

Gently muddle mint leaves from one sprig in the bottom of a mixing glass. Add the other ingredients. Add ice to the mixing glass and stir. Strain over fresh ice into a chilled rocks glass. Garnish with mint.

Farley Granger, James Stewart, and John Dall

Camembert in a Coffin

Our vision here is simple: a wheel of Camembert is lowered into a loaf of baked bread, stabbed with garlic slivers and rosemary needles, then warmed. Preparing it can be rather cathartic. Make sure to start with room-temperature cheese, or it will need a longer baking time. To present this dish, we like to wreath it with a variety of accompaniments that can be used for dipping or for stacking on crackers: celery sticks, sliced green apples or pears, water crackers or baguette rounds, walnuts, radishes, and cucumber rounds.

1 round loaf of baked yeasted bread (about 20 ounces)

1 8-ounce round of Camembert, room temperature

1 tablespoon white wine

2 to 3 garlic cloves, cut into slivers

1 small sprig rosemary, needles only

Preheat the oven to 300°F.

Use the Camembert box as a template to trace a circle on top of the bread with a paring knife. Once you've cut a circle, pry off the bread "lid" and core out as much of the bread as necessary so the Camembert can fit snugly down into the hole. Lower the cheese into the bread—it should be level.

Pierce about a dozen slits through the surface of the Camembert. Drizzle the wine over the surface—this will keep the rind from drying out—then, insert garlic slivers and rosemary needles into the slits. These will meld with the cheese as it warms.

Set the entombed Camembert onto a baking sheet, and lay the top of the bread beside it. Bake for 20 to 30 minutes, until the rosemary needles are gently browned and the cheese is soft to the touch. Serve warm. Note: The rind is edible, but if your guests are rind averse, just peel back the top of the cheese and let them spoon out the soft center.

The director and his stars

Parmigiano Rope Twists

These quick twists make use of the Moroccan spice blend ras el hanout, which plays nicely off this herbaceous cocktail. You can buy ras el hanout at a spice store or online, or you can find our recipe on page 77.

1 package (17.3 ounces) frozen puff pastry dough, thawed

1 egg, beaten and mixed with 1 tablespoon water

½ cup grated Parmigiano Reggiano, divided

2 tablespoons finely chopped parsley, divided

2 teaspoons ras el hanout or smoked paprika, divided

Preheat the oven to 400°F and line a pair of baking sheets with parchment paper.

Unroll each pastry sheet (there are two per box) on a pan and brush the surfaces with the egg mixture.

Sprinkle each sheet with ¼ cup Parmigiano, 1 tablespoon of parsley, and 1 teaspoon spice. Gently press these into the dough (a rolling pin works well).

Use a pizza roller or paring knife to cut each sheet into long strips, about ½-inch wide.

Lift and twist each strip, separating them on the tray by about an inch so they don't puff up and crowd one another.

Bake for 15 minutes, or until golden brown. Serve warm or at room temperature.

Set the Scene ◄◄◄◄◄

Silver candelabras with ivory candlesticks, a low centerpiece of white lilies, and a lace tablecloth are part of the "ceremonial alter" that evil geniuses Phillip (Farley Granger) and Brandon (John Dall) construct for the soiree in their ritzy New York apartment. Set out a buffet of snacks—or call it a potluck and ask everyone to bring a murderous dish. In the movie, you'll see a regal spread, including roast chicken (page 50) and paté (page 191), along with chocolate-covered sundaes topped with a cherry. The presentation is formal, served on silver trays. Appropriate attire: sport coats with pocket handkerchiefs. Don't forget to carry a bit of rope with you.

Behind the scenes of *Rope*

While You're Watching...

★ Notice how the light changes in the last third of the film, after the guests have departed. And, of course, keep an eye out for Alfred Hitchcock, who always makes a cameo. Hint: His trademark profile appears in neon.

★ *Rope* is adapted from a play of the same name. Playwright Patrick Hamilton based the story on two well-heeled Chicago law students who went on a crime binge, otherwise known as the Leopold and Loeb case of 1924.

ADAM'S RIB (1949)

Menu
CURRY FOR TWO

Lime Daiquiri

Cold Melon Halves (suggested)

Lamb Stew with Aromatic Rice

FEW THINGS ARE COZIER THAN A FRAGRANT POT OF CURRY ON the stove, which is exactly what appears in this groundbreaking romp starring Katharine Hepburn and Spencer Tracy. The two play a married couple, the Bonners—both are lawyers, who can be fierce in court but fawning at home. Together, they cook gourmet meals, trade massages, nuzzle on the couch, and ride to work in a fashionable convertible. When they get involved with a housewife (Judy Holliday) who shot her cheating husband, they end up on opposite sides of her case, which only enlivens their banter.

Based on a real court case, *Adam's Rib* has the feel of a film ahead of its time. Adam (Tracy) and Amanda (Hepburn) investigate marital inequality in the courtroom, then return home to share domestic duties like a pair of model mates in love and success. Their perfect world suggests that career couples can find bliss at work and at home, as long as that world also includes cocktails on the couch, fluffy robes, and occasional intellectual sparring. At the end of the movie, tempers flare—making a spicy curry most appropriate.

Opposite: **Dueling lawyers and lovers: Adam (Spencer Tracy) and Amanda (Katharine Hepburn)**

Lime Daiquiri

The original daiquiri hails from Cuba and made it to US shores in 1909, when it was brought to the Army Navy Club in Washington, D.C. From there, it went on to become one of the world's most popular drinks. Legend has it that Julian Cox, an engineer, ran out of his usual gin while entertaining guests and substituted local rum.

2 ounces light rum

1 ounce fresh lime juice

½ ounce simple syrup (1:1 sugar and water)

Lime wheel, for garnish

Shake ingredients with ice and strain into a chilled coupe glass, or serve in a tumbler over ice. Garnish with a lime wheel.

Above: **Enjoying breakfast in bed**

Lamb Stew with Aromatic Rice

This sweet and savory lamb curry made with butternut squash and apple is very autumnal. It's also very flexible—feel free to substitute chicken for lamb, or experiment with different vegetables, such as cauliflower, green beans, potatoes, or carrots. This dish is even better the second day, so you may want to make it the night before and gently warm it before serving.

SERVES 4

For the curry

1 pound lamb, cubed

1 tablespoon all-purpose white flour

1½ teaspoons garam masala

1½ teaspoons ground cumin

1 teaspoon ground turmeric

1 teaspoon salt

2 tablespoons extra-virgin olive oil

1 thumb of ginger, 2 inches long, peeled and grated

1 medium yellow onion, roughly chopped

2 cloves garlic, minced

2 Roma tomatoes, chopped

1 green chile, seeded and minced

1 pound butternut squash, peeled and cubed (about 2 cups)

1 green apple, peeled and chopped

1 cup apple cider

1 cup coconut milk

1 red bell pepper, seeded and chopped

2 cups fresh baby spinach, loosely packed

Roasted cashews, for garnish

Cilantro, for garnish

For the aromatic rice

2 tablespoons butter, divided

1 small onion, minced

2 cloves garlic, minced

1 cup basmati rice

1½ cups water or broth

1 bay leaf

1 cinnamon stick

⅓ cup white raisins

For the curry: Toss lamb cubes in a bowl with flour, spices, and salt and stir with a wooden spoon to coat. Heat oil in a Dutch oven or medium-size stew pot, and sear the meat over medium-high heat for 3 to 4 minutes, or until the edges begin to brown. Add ginger, onion, and garlic, and stir briefly to soften the onion, about 3 minutes. Toss in tomatoes, chile, squash, and apple, then add liquids. Simmer partially covered for 30 to 40 minutes, stirring from time to time. Taste and reseason with salt if needed.

Add the bell pepper 2 minutes before serving so that it softens but doesn't get soggy, then fold in spinach to wilt. Serve over rice, and top with cashews and chopped cilantro, with a dish of chutney, if desired.

For the rice: Start the rice once the curry is simmering, or about 30 minutes before you plan on eating. Melt 1 tablespoon of butter in a saucepan over medium heat, then add onion and garlic. Sauté for about 3 minutes, or until the onions are translucent, then add rice and water, spices, and raisins. Bring to a rolling boil, then lower the heat and cover. Simmer for 15 to 17 minutes, or until all the liquid is absorbed. Remove the pan from the heat and let stand (covered) for 10 minutes to finish steaming. Then remove the bay leaf and cinnamon, and add the remaining tablespoon of butter. Fluff with a fork and serve.

The Bonners hosting a dinner party

Set the Scene ❮❮❮❮❮❮

Intimate dining scenes are a highlight of this film, making this a prime movie for date night. *Adam's Rib* opens with breakfast in bed, followed by a tumble on the couch with daiquiris. The kitchen chemistry is most apparent when Hepburn and Tracy raid the refrigerator together to make dinner one evening after work—she in a floor-length houndstooth robe, he with an apron slung over his suit. As he makes a salad, she starts a lamb curry, and when they sit down for their first course—melon halves and tea at the kitchen table—an eccentric neighbor drops by to serenade them on the piano. Set the scene for a cozy supper, and don't forget your robes and slippers. For dessert, serve an assortment of candy bars ("chocolate nut bahs") and licorice—both are mentioned in the film.

While You're Watching...

★ Hepburn and Tracy had a decades-long love affair that started soon after they met on the set of *Woman of the Year* (1942) and lasted until Tracy's death in 1967.

★ This movie is all about married collaborators. The script was written by husband-wife team Ruth Gordon and Garson Kanin, who were intrigued by the real-life story of a set of married attorneys. In actuality, those attorneys ended up divorcing to marry their clients. (Interestingly, Ruth Gordon was also the actress who starred in *Harold and Maude*, 1971.)

★ Notice the pants Hepburn wears to court. They were deemed "sports slacks"—a popular fashion phenomenon after the film.

Right: **Spencer Tracy, Judy Holliday, and Katharine Hepburn**

"And, after you shot him, how did you feel then?" —AMANDA BONNER

"Hungry!" —DORIS ATTINGER

SUNSET BOULEVARD [1950]

Menu

OLD HOLLYWOOD

Ritz Cocktail

Smoked Oyster Waldorf Salad in Avocado Shells

Caviar Toasts

A HOLLYWOOD GOTHIC WITH MORE THAN A TOUCH OF CAMP, *SUNSET Boulevard* has been hailed as one of the greatest films ever made. No movie captures the vicissitudes of fame or the dark, garish life of a washed-up starlet like this masterpiece from director Billy Wilder. The film opens on a Hollywood mansion with a man's body floating in the pool. He turns out to be young, hard-up screenwriter Joe Gillis (William Holden) who wandered onto the grounds quite by accident. The mansion's resident, Norma Desmond (Gloria Swanson), is a wealthy older woman who once ruled the world of silent films. As the storyline carries us back in time, their unlikely relationship unfolds, one glistening web-like strand at a time.

It was Wilder's genius to cast Gloria Swanson in the role of Norma Desmond—herself a former silent screen star who did not successfully transition to talking pictures. She had even occupied a lavish house on Sunset Boulevard in the 1930s. Here she plays a spider-like beauty who lounges on sofas in sequins, surrounded by her own head shots, and interacts with almost no one, except for her cherished chauffeur. Gillis becomes her house cat. When he tries to slip away, well . . . you know what happens.

Incredible acting, opulent sets, and stunning film noir–like cinematography make this a thrill to watch.

Police pulling Joe Gillis's body out of the swimming pool

Ritz Cocktail

Created by famed bartender Dale Degroff in 1985, as a throwback to the glorious days of yore, this elegant drink pairs beautifully with any special occasion. The drink's backbone is Cognac, or brandy, making for a bubbly libation with class and a bit of heft.

¾ ounce brandy

½ ounce Cointreau

¼ ounce fresh lemon juice

¼ ounce Luxardo Maraschino Liqueur

2 ounces chilled Champagne (or Crémant)

Orange twist, for garnish

Stir the ingredients, except Champagne, with ice and strain into a martini glass. Top with Champagne and garnish with an orange twist on the rim of the glass.

Above: **Gloria Swanson as Norma Desmond**

Smoked Oyster Waldorf Salad in Avocado Shells

Glamorous and a little outré, this is the ideal recipe to match Norma Desmond's histrionic personality. Do not fear the smoked oysters. They perform admirably here giving this version of the famed Waldorf Salad (the favorite of divas everywhere) excellent depth of flavor and a bit of added interest. Just be sure the avocados are nicely ripe.

SERVES 6

1 cup walnuts

3 large avocados, ripe but firm

2 tablespoons lemon juice

3 tablespoons mayonnaise

3 tablespoons sour cream

1 rib celery, finely chopped

1 tin (3 ounces) smoked oysters, drained and halved

1 red apple, cored and finely chopped (Cortland or Honeycrisp)

Salad greens, washed and dried

Freshly ground black pepper, for garnish

6 lemon wedges, for garnish

Toast the walnuts in a dry skillet or in the oven. Cool and break into pieces.

Cut the avocados in half lengthwise and remove the pit. Using a large spoon, scoop out the flesh and cut into small cubes, reserving the shells.

In a small mixing bowl, combine the avocado, lemon juice, mayonnaise, sour cream, celery, oysters, and apple. Stir. Cover the mixture and refrigerate for 15 to 20 minutes so the flavors can meld. Before serving, fold in the walnuts.

To present this dish, mound the chilled salad into the reserved avocado shells and set each one on a bed of greens. Garnish with freshly ground pepper and a lemon wedge.

Caviar Toasts (PHOTO ON PAGE 106)

Petit toasts topped with crème fraîche and caviar? Why not? Look for sustainable American Sturgeon or Paddlefish caviar. Or, substitute less expensive fish eggs, like salmon or tobiko. The salty eggs are a perfect foil for the Champagne cocktail as well as Waldorf salad.

Set the Scene ◄◄◄◄◄◄

Robes, rhinestones, turbans, tails—your most self-indulgent and eccentric attire is required here. Break out the leopard print, hang a bed sheet as a dramatic drape, and let out your inner diva—not the YouTube-popstar kind—but the real, operatic, crazy aunt, thrift-store variety. Since Norma Desmond undergoes an extensive beauty regime during the second half of this film, it's worth breaking out the mud masks and sending around a tray of damp, warm wash cloths (moisten them, roll them, and Crock-Pot them for a couple hours on low) alongside a second round of drinks.

While You're Watching ...

★ Desmond's butler, Max, is played by none other than director Erich von Stroheim, who directed actress Gloria Swanson in silent films.

★ The photos displayed around Desmond's house are the real photos of Gloria Swanson from her heyday in the 1920s, when she starred in *Zaza* (1923), *Madame Sans-Gene* (1925), and *The Untamed Lady* (1926).

★ Montgomery Clift quit the role of Joe since he was, in real life, dating the wealthy older actress Libby Holman.

Norma Desmond (Swanson) desperately holding on to Joe (William Holden)

AN AMERICAN IN PARIS (1951)

Menu

FRENCH PICNIC

American in Paris Cocktail

Cheese Board with Charcuterie
and Dijon Mustard

Baguette and Chocolate (suggested)

CHARM ALERT. If you're yearning for Paris, feeling lackluster, or dreaming of a little soiree with wine and runny cheese, well, *mes chéries*, you are in luck. In this musical, Gene Kelly plays an American G.I. turned painter who resides in an adorable Parisian apartment overlooking a cobblestoned street. He saunters through markets in linen slacks, falls for a kitten-ish girl (Leslie Caron) who works at a perfume counter, paints en plein air, and does his best to avoid being seduced by a wealthy art collector (Nina Foch) who wants to become his sexy patron.

Full of kinetic dance scenes and magnificent Gershwin tunes, *An American in Paris* is the sort of film that makes you want to drop out of life and rent a room on the Left Bank. No wonder it ate up so many Oscars in 1951, including Best Costume, Best Score, Best Screenplay—and, of course—Best Picture. Critics' darling *A Streetcar Named Desire* didn't have a chance against this sunny valentine.

Prepare to hum "Swonderful, smarvelous . . ." all night long. This elegant musical should be enjoyed with good friends, travel partners, or Francophiles who adore cheese and wine.

Opposite: **Gene Kelly waving from the window of his Paris apartment**

An American in Paris Cocktail

Think of this as a brambly Manhattan that pairs well with slightly funky cheese. Tart and woodsy, it's a perfect blend of American spirit (bourbon) and French taste (currant liqueur, or cassis). If you want to mix things up, offer Champagne Cocktails (page 232), which appear early in the film, along with Martinis (page 41) and sherry. Use a good dry vermouth here, like Noilly Prat.

1½ ounces bourbon

½ ounce crème de cassis

½ ounce dry vermouth

½ ounce fresh lemon juice

Half a lemon slice, for garnish

Combine ingredients in a shaker over ice. Shake and strain into a chilled cocktail glass. Garnish with half a lemon slice floating on the surface.

Nina Foch and Gene Kelly sipping cocktails in her apartment

Cheese Board with Charcuterie and Dijon Mustard

Within 10 minutes of watching this film, you'll see market baguettes and warm brioche buns. Make sure to feature a decadent breadbasket alongside three to five French cheeses, all of which pair beautifully with this film's signature cocktail. If there are wine drinkers in the crowd, offer wine pairings (provided in our discussion of cheeses). We like to serve these cheeses in courses throughout the film so that guests can explore signature French pairings, but you can also set up a grand cheese board and let everyone graze. Be sure to reserve a baguette to serve with dark chocolate at the end as a palate cleanser. Note: The French cheeses we've selected are easy to find at quality cheese counters. Don't sweat it if you can't find one or two—just pluck a cheese in the same style, or ask a cheesemonger to suggest something similar.

Valençay

This beautiful pyramid-shaped goat cheese predates Charlemagne. It's terrific with a Loire Valley white, like Sauvignon Blanc. Serve it on a plate surrounded by blackberries and a dish of light-colored honey or raw honeycomb. For a savory starter, serve it with steamed asparagus dressed with a drizzle of olive oil and a pinch of lemon zest.

Delice de Bourgogne

A triple crème made just outside Paris, this is one of the most luxe cheeses you can buy stateside. Pair it with Champagne and sour cherry preserves, or swing savory with wild mushrooms sautéed in butter and a fistful of chopped chives. Serve with toasted brioche or baguette rounds.

Epoisses

One of France's whiffiest cheeses, Epoisses is actually illegal to carry on French trains. Don't be a coward! Unless this umber-colored round (sold in a balsa wood box) is supremely ripe, the smell is inoffensive. And the taste is beyond words, like creamed onions and bacon. Before you serve it, uncover it and let it breathe for an hour (the smell will dissipate). Serve with warm, steamed new potatoes, celery sticks, and toasted baguette rounds. White Burgundy is an exquisite pairing.

Comté

Pair this sweet, nutty Alpine cheese with caramelized nuts, Dijon mustard, onion jam, and pickles. A good sausage, like saucisson sec, is marvelous alongside. Comté is one of the great cave-aged cheeses of all time. It melts beautifully on toast or over French onion soup, if you want to try it in place of Gruyère—which is a cousin to this cheese, but more savory instead of brightly sweet. For the perfect wine pairing, seek out an Arbois Chardonnay; but a nice dry Chardonnay will do.

Roquefort

One of the world's best blue cheeses, this luxurious cave-aged sheep's milk blue needs ripe pears, walnuts, and honey. Serve it on a board, or present it on individual dessert plates with slivers of Roquefort instead of cake. This is a great cheese to serve with the film's finale dance sequence, along with small chilled glasses of Sauternes. The pairing is all honeyed fruit and minerals. Impossibly gorgeous. Your guests will be moved to float around the room.

"When I'm broke I don't eat. Then I get tired and depressed. When that happens, the only thing that helps is wine and women."

—JERRY MULLIGAN

How to Arrange a Cheese Board

Use one large board and stagger the cheeses along it in the order listed (they should be eaten from mildest to strongest, as presented here). Fill in around them with berries, dried fruit, nuts, honey, and jam (rhubarb, apricot, or berry). For garnish, insert sprigs of fresh rosemary. This looks especially nice around cured meats, like a rustic saucisson sec served with a jar of Dijon mustard.

You can prepare the cheese board an hour or two before guests arrive and let it sit out so the cheeses reach room temperature. If you're worried about them drying out, drape them with a large piece of damp cheesecloth. The effect is dramatic and makes for a spectacular unveiling. For a festive, cocktail-driven presentation, try serving toasted baguette rounds in martini glasses.

Set the Scene ◄◄◄◄◄◄

Tie a kerchief around your neck, à la Gene Kelly, and toss a checkered tablecloth over the coffee table. This meal is all about the cheese board. To set the scene, incorporate an easel with paintbrushes, and consider serving a round of Champagne Cocktails (page 232) when guests arrive. Dress should be Parisian casual: striped nautical tops, black turtlenecks and berets, or wide-collared shirts with tweed jackets (you'll want to carry a pipe in the pocket). We like to serve mugs of onion soup with a little Cognac at the end of this viewing, if we are watching in winter. Otherwise, we round out the cheese board with a light salad early on and add a tray of meringues and fresh berries during the final epic ballet (see note on the next page).

Above: **Leslie Caron and Gene Kelly** | *Opposite:* Kelly and Caron in the final dance scene

While You're Watching...

★ The young lead opposite Gene Kelly? A French teenager he spotted on a Paris stage. *An American in Paris* is Leslie Caron's film debut, with a decades-long career before the camera to follow.

★ The final dance scene is 17 minutes long and cost almost half a million dollars, a small fortune at the time. The backdrops and costumes draw inspiration from different painters, including (in this order) Raoul Dufy, Auguste Renoir, Maurice Utrillo, Henri Rousseau, Vincent Van Gogh, and Henri de Toulouse-Lautrec.

★ Little-known fact: Gene Kelly dropped out of law school to pursue his dance career. A Pittsburgh native, his family owned a dance studio in the Squirrel Hill neighborhood, where Kelly taught throughout college. He became famous for his athletic style of dancing and choreography and for transforming the image of the tuxedo-clad tap dancer—epitomized by Fred Astaire—into a more relaxed character. Rolled up sleeves were a Kelly signature.

ROMAN HOLIDAY (1953)

Menu

A CAFÉ IN THE PIAZZA

Aperol Spritz

Crown of Cantaloupe Salad with Mozzarella Pearls

Baked Garlic Crostini

Gelato (suggested)

AUDREY HEPBURN MADE HER HOLLYWOOD SCREEN DEBUT AS Princess Ann, a darling but deeply unhappy royal who longs to experience a single day as an anonymous civilian in Rome. When she sneaks away from her guards, she meets reporter Joe Bradley (Gregory Peck), who treats her to a day of normal life among the people—drinks, dancing, gelato, her first cigarette, and a nervy swerve-y Vespa ride through crowded city streets. Her exuberance during this day-long romance is infectious, and Bradley grows smitten, even though he is secretly having her photographed by a member of the local paparazzi (Eddie Albert) for a story he plans to write.

If you've never seen Hepburn's first film, you'll be absolutely charmed. This is unfiltered Audrey, before most movie fans had even heard of her. Paramount picked Hepburn as a cost-saving device when director William Wyler signed on and insisted he film in Italy, a great expense. No one anticipated that Hepburn would become a mega star, much less an Oscar winner! Audiences were dazzled by her impishness and by her on-screen chemistry with Peck. In an era of bodacious blondes, Hepburn's girlish physique and simple style inspired legions of young women to imitate her.

With beautiful shots of Rome in the 1950s, *Roman Holiday* captures the post-war optimism of the time. It's light-hearted and vibrant, despite being shot in black and white (another cost-saving device). Make like a local and sip on an Aperol Spritz. Then pretend you are in a piazza by the fountain—sun blazing, church bells ringing—surrounded by high Italian fashion and classic architecture.

Opposite: **Audrey Hepburn as Princess Ann**

Aperol Spritz

Around 4 o'clock, cafés in Rome begin serving this sunset-colored cocktail made with Prosecco and the Italian aperitif Aperol. It's a low-proof libation that makes everyone feel social, and restaurants almost always offer complimentary bar bites: bruschetta or, quite often, a trio of small dishes containing potato chips, nuts, and plump green olives. Nobody does happy hour like the Italians.

1 ounce Aperol

3 ounces Prosecco

Splash of soda water (about ½ ounce)

Half an orange slice, for garnish

Fill a wine glass (or a highball glass, if you prefer) half-full of ice. Add Aperol, then Prosecco. Top off with a splash of soda water. Stir briefly, then drop in the orange slice or affix it to the edge of the glass.

Audrey Hepburn and Gregory Peck

" . . . First wish? One sidewalk café, comin' right up. I know just the place."

—JOE BRADLEY

Crown of Cantaloupe Salad with Mozzarella Pearls

Of the many variations on a Caprese, this combination of cool melon, salty prosciutto, and plush mozzarella is extra special. Fit for a princess? Naturally. The base of this salad is made with a ring of cantaloupe, topped with gem-like mozzarella pearls. Serve it alongside cocktails and Baked Garlic Crostini (page 123) for a light meal or snack.

SERVES 6

1 ripe cantaloupe

¼ pound prosciutto, loosely torn

3 cups arugula

1 tub (8 ounces) fresh mozzarella pearls (*ciliegini*), drained

12 basil leaves, sliced into ribbons

¼ cup sherry vinegar

6 tablespoons extra-virgin olive oil

1 tablespoon lemon zest

Salt and freshly ground black pepper, to taste

To peel the cantaloupe, trim the ends so you can see the seed bed, then use a paring knife to slice away the rind, making sure to remove any green color and any of the flesh that feels tough. Use a metal spoon to core out the seeds. Slice the cantaloupe crosswise, into ½-inch rounds.

Heat a large skillet and fry the prosciutto like bacon over medium heat. When the edges are crisp, after about 5 minutes, remove the prosciutto onto a plate to cool.

To assemble the salads, set out six salad plates. Place a handful of arugula on each plate and spread it out to make a base, then add a ring of cantaloupe in the center. Sprinkle the frizzled prosciutto around the edge, then nest the mozzarella pearls in the middle—you will have some mozzarella left over.

Top with basil ribbons. Give each salad a drizzle of vinegar (about 2 teaspoons each) and olive oil (1 tablespoon each). Add a pinch of lemon zest on top of the mozzarella, followed by a sprinkle of salt and some freshly ground pepper.

Baked Garlic Crostini

Because we like something interactive with our meals, we often serve roasted garlic as an appetizer. It's easy, and it's fun to incorporate whatever fresh herbs you have lying around as an accent. Here, we use rosemary (sometimes we tuck a few sprigs under the garlic), but you can also use fresh oregano, thyme, or even dried red pepper flakes.

SERVES 6

2 or 3 whole heads of garlic

4 tablespoons extra-virgin olive oil

2 teaspoons fresh rosemary (or 1 teaspoon dried)

Freshly ground black pepper

1 baguette, sliced into rounds, brushed with olive oil, and toasted

Sea salt, to taste

Preheat the oven to 400°F.

Trim the garlic crosswise, to expose the tops of the cloves embedded within, then set the heads cut-side up in an oven-safe crock, like a ramekin. Drizzle olive oil over each bulb, and top with rosemary and a few cranks of black pepper.

Wrap the crock in foil so that it is tightly sealed, then bake the garlic for 30 to 40 minutes, or until the cloves feel soft.

Serve warm with toasted baguette rounds and a dish of sea salt.

Set the Scene ◄◄◄◄◄

Roman Holiday is a dreamy film, perfect for a honeymoon-planning party, a group of globetrotting friends, or anyone with a yen for Italy and 1950s fashion. Set a cool, breezy tone at the table with stone candlesticks, linen napkins, earthenware, and maybe a potted succulent. Play up bleached colors and natural beauty. Postcards for invitations? Why not? If you want to add a main course, try our Bowtie Pasta with Spicy Vodka Cream Sauce (page 35).

While You're Watching...

★ Gregory Peck was so blown away by Hepburn's performance while they were filming that he insisted her name be listed above his in the credits. He also predicted her Oscar win.

★ Screenwriter Dalton Trumbo was not listed in this film's credits because at the time he was blacklisted for his ties to the Communist Party. He couldn't even collect the Academy Award for Best Story that the film won. Sixty years later, Trumbo's name was finally added to the opening credits in bold letters—thanks, in part, to his son's advocacy.

Above: **The journalist and the princess** | *Opposite:* **Joe Bradley showing the princess around Rome**

GUYS AND DOLLS (1955)

Menu

DINNER IN HAVANA

Coconut Milk Punch

Arroz con Pollo

Bakery Cheesecake
(suggested)

MARLON BRANDO, SINGING. That might be reason enough to give this well-acted, brilliantly choreographed musical a look, but from the very first color-saturated scene set in pre-Disneyfied Times Square, the witty dialogue, catchy tunes, and engaging storyline are mighty hooks. Gambler Nathan Detroit (Frank Sinatra) is short $1,000 dollars to host a craps game. He bets Sky Masterson (Marlon Brando) that he can't take cold fish Sergeant Sarah Brown (Jean Simmons) for dinner in Havana. Through uproarious scenes (bar fight!) and sexy show tunes (kitty meow song!), the comedy ends with a double wedding between Nathan and his longtime mistress (played wonderfully by Vivian Blaine) as well as the unlikely sinner Sky Masterson and salvation-seeking Sergeant Brown.

Left: **Double wedding in Times Square**

Based on a hit Broadway play, *Guys and Dolls* was Brando's first and last musical role, and while Gene Kelly might have been a natural fit here, Brando was the era's box-office sizzler. The actor so well known for dramatic performances in *A Streetcar Named Desire* (1951) and *On the Waterfront* (1954) hated the sound of his singing voice (he compared it to "the mating call of a yak") and spent hours working with voice coaches and recording multiple takes, which were then patched together for the movie. Meanwhile, Sinatra—known for his singing roles—sat around disgusted. Let's just say: Brando's baby face and cool delivery more than make up for his crooning, which is *prettttty* smooth—not unlike our coconut milk punch.

Set the Scene ◄◄◄◄◄◄

Cue the Cuban jazz and get ready to roll some dice. This movie is all about dancing and gambling. We like to serve the cocktails before the meal and then bring out a bottle of dry Spanish wine for the main dish. If you want a splurge for dessert, pick up a cheesecake from a local bakery—and since it's featured early in the movie, go ahead and eat dessert first. You could even spoon some dulce de leche over the top.

Above: **Brando rolling dice in the sewer** | *Opposite:* **Marlon Brando and Jean Simmons**

While You're Watching…

★ Frank Sinatra had to a take a day off from filming *Guys and Dolls* when he became physically ill after Marlon Brando deliberately goofed his lines over and over during the scene in which Sinatra eats a piece of cheesecake (which revolted him). The two actors did not get along and, by the end of the shoot, were no longer on speaking terms.

★ *Guys and Dolls* was adapted from a collection of Damon Runyon short stories. Runyon was famous for depicting colorful (some might say "seedy") New York characters—hustlers, gangsters, Broadway actors—and for nailing their speech patterns. His style of dialogue has been dubbed "Runyonese."

Above: **Frank Sinatra and Vivian Blaine** | *Opposite:* **Enjoying "Dulce de Leche" cocktails**

Coconut Milk Punch

The turning point of the romance between Masterson and Brown happens over—what else?—a few drinks. Brando orders a cocktail called Dulce de Leche, which arrives in a hollowed-out coconut shell. Brown gets drunk, the couple has dinner, dances, brawls with the locals, and falls in love. A good first date! The problem is, there's no such drink as the Dulce de Leche. The closest thing in 1950s Havana would have been the Doncellita, a concoction of coffee liqueur and evaporated milk. But, there is a kind of Caribbean Coconut Milk Punch, also made with evaporated milk, which employs the "preservative" Bacardi, as Masterson slyly calls it.

SERVES 4

2 cups coconut water

1 cup evaporated milk (a 12-ounce can contains 1½ cups)

1 cup light or gold rum

3 tablespoons granulated sugar

1 teaspoon ground cinnamon

½ teaspoon freshly grated nutmeg

Combine ingredients in a jar or pitcher. Stir. Refrigerate until cold, about 1 hour. Pour into chilled rocks glasses over cubes or crushed ice. Serve with a straw.

Tip: This drink can be made using four fresh coconuts. Hollow out the eyes, drain the coconut water (should be about the necessary 2 cups), and hack open for serving.

Arroz con Pollo

The scene where Masterson and Brown are eating at the El Café Cabana shows Jean Simmons taking a couple of forkfuls of rice. In 1950s Havana, a classic special-occasion dish would have been arroz con pollo, or chicken with rice. This easy one-pot meal is a cinch to make before the movie, and it is filling enough for a small hoard of hungry gamblers. Serve with a simple side salad of your choice.

SERVES 6 TO 8

¼ cup extra-virgin olive oil

4 pounds chicken thighs, bone in (about 9 or 10 pieces)

2 medium onions, chopped

1 medium red bell pepper, chopped

5 medium cloves garlic, minced

1 bay leaf

1 teaspoon ground cumin

1 teaspoon dried oregano

1 teaspoon freshly ground black pepper

1 tablespoon salt

Juice of 1 lemon (about 3 tablespoons)

2 cups chicken stock

2 tablespoons tomato paste

¼ teaspoon red pepper flakes

6 saffron strands

2 cups uncooked short-grain white rice (Valencia)

1 bottle (12 ounces) beer (lager)

1 cup dry white wine

1 cup baby peas, fresh or frozen

2 limes, cut in wedges, for garnish

¼ cup large capers, for garnish

Heat olive oil in a Dutch oven or stew pot over medium-high heat. Working in batches, add chicken and brown on both sides, about 4 minutes per side. Remove each batch to a plate and set aside.

Lower heat to medium and add onions and red pepper, stirring until onions are translucent, about 5 minutes. Then, add the garlic, bay leaf, cumin, oregano, black pepper, salt, and lemon juice. Stir briefly to combine.

Add the chicken stock, tomato paste, red pepper flakes, saffron, and rice. Stir to combine. Return chicken to the pot. Add beer and wine. The chicken should be submerged in liquid; if not, top with more wine. Bring the pot to a simmer, then cook uncovered on low for 30 minutes, or until the rice is tender.

Five minutes before serving, add the peas. Remove the pan from heat and serve in shallow bowls with limes and capers for garnish.

"You want to take me to dinner in Havana, Cuba?" —SERGEANT SARAH BROWN

"Well, they eat in Cuba the same as we do." —SKY MASTERSON

GIANT (1956)

Menu

A TEXAS WELCOME

Chocolate Martini

Barbacoa with Tortillas, Onions, and Cilantro

TODAY MARFA, TEXAS—THE LOCATION WHERE *GIANT* WAS SHOT— is known for its international art scene and its fake Prada store sculpture, but in the 1950s it was a pile of dust. Imagine sultry young beauty Elizabeth Taylor and beefcake Rock Hudson bored out of their gourds on the set of *Giant*. Legend has it, that's when they created the chocolate martini together, comprised of vodka, Kahlua, and Hershey's chocolate syrup—they both loved martinis and chocolate. Taylor even includes the recipe in her diet cookbook, *Elizabeth Takes Off* (1988).

What better cocktail to pair with *barbacoa*, or Mexican pit-roasted meat, from which the term "barbecue" is derived? It appears early in the film, when Leslie Benedict (Taylor) arrives in Texas as a new bride to Jordan "Bick" Benedict II (Hudson) and meets her husband's neighbors. They treat her to a proper ranch supper, a meal that serves as her initiation. Determined to fit in, she retires her East Coast party dress for a horsewoman's attire, but she never relinquishes her feisty spirit. Throughout the story, she rules as a sharp-talking beauty and challenges her stony husband to treat those around him with more humanity.

Giant was one of three films directed by George Stevens in the 1950s that explore the American dream (along with *A Place in the Sun* and *Shane*). It was also James Dean's last performance. True to the method acting technique he was known for, Dean got locals to show him how to handle a lasso and how to wear his hat, so that he could appear authentic. His role as a farm hand turned oil-rich eccentric suits him well here. He's both magnetic and off-putting, just as he was in real life.

Opposite: **Elizabeth Taylor and James Dean**

Set the Scene

The scope of *Giant* is epic—it begins in the 1920s, then advances through World War II. Pick an era to highlight, or keep it simple with a cactus centerpiece, rustic serving ware, and a selection of bourbons. Since this movie is long, we like to take "bourbon breaks" along the way. You can even suggest a bourbon tasting to your guests in advance and invite them to bring a bottle. Note that Tom and Jerrys (page 151) appear in the second half of the film, during a Christmas scene.

While You're Watching…

★ Notice all the "J. R." references in the second half of the film. The character of Jett Rink (James Dean) was the inspiration behind the television series *Dallas* and its protagonist J. R. Ewing, played by Larry Hagman.

★ *Giant* was based on Edna Ferber's 416-page novel about the life of a Texas oil tycoon. She also wrote *Show Boat* (1926), which was adapted into a major musical, and *Cimarron* (1929), which was turned into a film (it won an Academy Award for Best Picture in 1931).

★ James Dean was killed in a car accident on September 30, 1955—four days after he finished filming his final scenes.

Chocolate Martini

This drink's sugary effect is a perfect counter-balance to Giant's stark Texas landscape. If you prefer a more masculine sip, set out a bottle of bourbon—it pairs with Hudson's signature line: "Just remember, one of these days, that bourbon's gonna kill you" to which Chill Wills replies, "Okay, it'll be me or it. One of us has to go."

2 ounces vodka 2 ounces Kahlua 2 squirts (about 1 ounce) Hershey's Chocolate Syrup	Pour ingredients into an ice-filled shaker. Shake, then strain into a chilled martini glass.

Above: **James Dean and Elizabeth Taylor** | *Opposite:* **James Dean as Jett Rink**

"You sure do look pretty, Miss Leslie. Pert nigh good enough to eat!" —JETT RINK

Barbacoa with Tortillas, Onions, and Cilantro

The big Texas welcome in Giant *includes pit-roasted beef, barbacoa. But face-to-face with the entire head of a cow, Leslie (Taylor) faints. The episode steels her resolve to conquer her new homeland. This recipe makes for flavorful and rich barbacoa with serious depth of flavor. For those who like things spicier, this preparation will respond to extra heat nicely. Just keep those hot sauces at the ready. Note that the meat needs time to marinate, so consider prepping this the night before.*

SERVES 6 TO 8

2 to 3 yellow onions (1 pound), peeled and diced

8 medium garlic cloves, minced

4 chipotle peppers packed in adobo, chopped

1 cup chicken stock

¼ cup apple cider vinegar

¼ cup fresh lime juice (2 to 3 limes)

2 teaspoons fish sauce

2 teaspoons dried thyme

2 teaspoons ground cumin

2 teaspoons dried Mexican oregano

1 teaspoon freshly ground black pepper

2 dried bay leaves

4 ground cloves (¼ teaspoon)

1 beef chuck or roast (4 to 5 pounds)

18 to 24 corn tortillas (3 per serving)

1 small white onion, diced, for garnish

1 small bunch cilantro, chopped, for garnish

In a large roasting pan that will fit in your fridge, combine onions, garlic, chipotle peppers, chicken stock, apple cider vinegar, lime juice, fish sauce, thyme, cumin, oregano, black pepper, bay leaves, and cloves. Add the beef and turn to coat. Seal the pan with foil and let it rest in the refrigerator for 4 hours or overnight, turning occasionally.

Preheat the oven to 300°F. Cook the meat, covered, about 4 to 5 hours, or until it's tender. Remove it from the oven, discard the foil, and let the meat rest for 10 minutes.

Using two forks, pull the meat apart and set it on a lipped plate or serving dish.

Serve with warm corn tortillas, white onions, and cilantro.

SOME LIKE
IT HOT (1959)

Menu
DINNER WITH A MILLIONAIRE

Manhattan

Saltines with Peanut Butter (suggested)

Manhattan-Marinated Flank Steak

Velvet Potatoes

F ULL OF MUSICAL NUMBERS, MIXED DRINKS, CROSS-DRESSING, AND gangsters, *Some Like It Hot* has everything you could want for an evening's laugh riot. Joe (Tony Curtis) and Jerry (Jack Lemmon) are two jazz musicians from Chicago who accidentally witness the infamous mobster bloodbath known as the Valentine's Day Massacre. Discovered by the mob, they flee by boarding a Miami-bound train and scheme their way into an all-girl band—by assuming new identities as Josephine and Daphne!

Such is the setup for one of the most uproarious comedies of all time. Also on the train is the band's singer and ukulele player, Sugar Kane (Marilyn Monroe), a chanteuse who enjoys a little too much bourbon with her plucking. During the infamous pajama party scene, Monroe's character mixes Manhattans in her berth by shaking up cocktails in a hot water bottle, the inspiration for our meal. Josephine and Daphne compete for her attention throughout the film, playing up their "feminine" sensibilities to earn Sugar's trust when the band settles in Florida. She, meanwhile, has her sights set on marrying a yacht-dwelling millionaire.

Opposite: **Marilyn Monroe with Tony Curtis and Jack Lemmon in drag**

Under Billy Wilder's direction, Curtis and Lemmon perform flawlessly as a comic duo, and Monroe, who was notoriously difficult on set (partly due to the fact that she was pregnant), makes one of her most beloved appearances. In honor of this epic romp, we present not just a Manhattan, but a Manhattan-marinated steak. It's decadent and delicious, the consummate pairing for a night of over-the-top entertainment.

Set the Scene ◄◄◄◄◄

To give the feel of Florida in the late 1950s, find a wild botanical-print tablecloth or use a wool beach blanket, and strew shells across it. We like to serve Manhattans and saltines with peanut butter at the start of this movie, to pair it with the scene where they appear. Serve another round of cocktails alongside the steaks, or switch to a full-bodied red, such as a Syrah. If you want to offer dessert, make it a pie—key lime or lemon meringue. Or try a Pineapple Sundae (page 169).

While You're Watching…

★ Because Monroe was pregnant during the making of the film, stand-ins posed for the movie's stills and her head was superimposed on the bodies.

★ The Florida scenes were actually shot in California at the Coronado Hotel. Look closely and you can see mountains in the background.

"I don't care how rich he is, as long as he has a yacht, his own private railroad car, and his own toothpaste."

—SUGAR

Above: **Marilyn Monroe** | *Opposite:* **Marilyn Monroe with Tony Curtis**

Manhattan

Early proportions of this classic cocktail would have been 1:1, but here we relate a modern 2:1 take so that the whiskey shines. Try using a high-proof rye whiskey, such as Rittenhouse, or a rough-around-the-edges classic, such as Old Overholt. For sweet vermouth, Carpano Antica is one of our favorites. For your garnish, quality bourbon-soaked cherries do make a difference.

2 ounces rye whiskey

1 ounce sweet vermouth

2 dashes Angostura bitters

Maraschino cherry, for garnish

Stir ingredients with ice and strain into a chilled coupe glass. Or, serve in a rocks glass with a large ice cube. Garnish with a cherry.

Tony Curtis and
Jack Lemmon

Manhattan-Marinated Flank Steak (PHOTO ON PAGE 144)

A steak marinated in a cocktail? Why not? After all, if Marilyn can make a Manhattan in a hot water bottle, why not take it a step further? Here, we invert the ratio of sweet vermouth to rye and add just a little soy sauce to up the umami. The result is tender steak with rich flavor. You can toss it on the grill, or sear it in a skillet and finish it in the oven, as we do here. Feel free to double or triple the recipe to include friends; we kept the portions small, in case you want to enjoy a cozy supper, as Sugar does with her million-dollar man.

SERVES 2

For the marinade

1 ounce bourbon or rye

2 ounces sweet vermouth

4 dashes Angostura bitters

2 teaspoons extra-virgin olive oil

1 teaspoon soy sauce

1 teaspoon dark brown sugar

For the steak

1 flank steak (1 pound, about 1½ inches thick)

Salt and freshly ground black pepper

1 tablespoon extra-virgin olive oil

1 tablespoon unsalted butter

For the finishing sauce

1 small shallot, finely chopped

1 tablespoon all-purpose white flour

1 cup beef broth, warmed

2 tablespoons heavy cream

Blue cheese (optional), for garnish (like Gorgonzola Piccante)

Prepare the marinade by whisking the ingredients together in a small bowl. Then season your steak with salt and pepper on both sides and drop it into a large resealable plastic bag. Pour the marinade over it. Seal the bag and set it in a bowl (in case it leaks) and refrigerate for about two hours.

Bring the steak to room temperature for 30 minutes before cooking (you can just leave it in the bag on your counter). Then position a rack in the center of your oven and preheat to 350°F.

Heat an oven-safe skillet over medium-high heat and when a water droplet sizzles on the surface, add olive oil, then butter (this will keep the butter from browning). Add the steak to the pan, reserving the leftover marinade for the finishing sauce. Sear the steak for 4 minutes without touching it. When you flip it, it should be nice and brown. Sear the second side for 4 minutes.

Transfer the skillet to the oven to finish cooking the steak—cooking time will vary depending on the thickness, but plan on approximately 15 minutes for medium rare, 20 minutes for medium, and 25 for well-done.

Remove the skillet from the oven and transfer the steak to a cutting board. Cover it with foil while you prepare the finishing sauce.

For the finishing sauce, add the marinade and shallots to the hot skillet over medium heat. Cook, stirring, for 5 minutes, then stir in flour. Whisk in the broth—add it in a slow stream. Simmer 3 to 5 minutes, or until it has reduced to about half the original amount of liquid, stirring constantly. Lower the heat and stir in the cream. Taste to see if it needs more salt and pepper.

To serve the steak, slice it against the grain and spoon the sauce over each serving. Top with blue cheese, if desired.

Velvet Potatoes (PHOTO ON PAGE 144)

For these velvety scalloped potatoes, be sure to use waxy-skinned potatoes (like Yukon Gold). The result will be a melt-in-your mouth dish that pairs swimmingly with steak. Begin cooking the steak about 1 hour after the potatoes go into the oven.

SERVES 4

6 medium-size waxy white potatoes (about 2 pounds), peeled

3 tablespoons unsalted butter

1 small onion, finely chopped

2 cloves garlic, chopped

1½ teaspoons salt

½ teaspoon freshly ground black pepper

3 tablespoons all-purpose white flour

2 cups milk, warmed

½ cup dry white wine

1 teaspoon fresh thyme

2 teaspoons Dijon mustard

1 bay leaf

Preheat the oven to 350°F and butter a low, 2-quart casserole pan. Slice potatoes thinly and layer them in the pan so that they overlap in several rows.

In a medium-size saucepan, melt the butter over medium heat and add onion and garlic. Stir about 5 minutes, or until translucent. Then whisk in salt, pepper, and flour. Slowly whisk in the milk, then the wine. Add the thyme, mustard, and bay leaf. Bring to a simmer, stirring constantly, until mixture begins to thicken.

Pour the mixture over potatoes and cover with foil. Bake for 30 minutes. Uncover and bake 60 minutes more, or until potatoes are tender. Let stand 10 minutes before serving.

THE APARTMENT (1960)

Menu

HOLIDAY HOSPITALITY

Rum Collins and Tom and Jerry

Mixed Nuts and Cheese Crackers (suggested)

Build-Your-Own Turkey and Cranberry Club Sandwiches

BEST PICTURE OSCAR-WINNER *THE APARTMENT* IS ONE OF THE MOST endearing films about Manhattan, despite the fact that it explores the vices of a *Mad Men*-esque insurance company full of womanizing executives. Several of the bosses manipulate a young clerk, C. C. Baxter (Jack Lemmon) into lending them the key to his flat so that they can cavort with their secretaries before commuting home to their wives. Shirley MacLaine plays the company's elevator girl, and she—like Baxter—is trying to rise from the ground floor with her integrity intact. The challenge drives them both to extremes in a bittersweet comedy that is full of office parties and bachelor-pad suppers, including a spectacular scene where Baxter strains spaghetti through a tennis racket. Talk about a great kitchen hack.

Inspired by the many food references in this film, we turn to a few classic recipes for a casual holiday supper. If you happen to be the recipient of a fruitcake, this is your chance to set it out for snacking. It appears in the film, along with chicken noodle soup, spaghetti with meatballs, Martinis (page 41), Daiquiris (page 99), Champagne, a Rum Collins, and a reference to Tom and Jerrys. There's also a great scene at the beginning that features a TV dinner; Baxter peels back the foil on his meal and munches on a chicken drumstick while watching *Grand Hotel* (page 21), a perfect choice for a double feature.

BROADWAY

Shirley MacLaine and Jack Lemmon

Rum Collins

This terrifically simple variation on a Tom Collins—made with gin and lemon—is perfect around the holidays, and it tastes divine alongside a turkey club. In place of a cherry, we like to skewer a cranberry.

1½ ounces gold rum

½ ounce fresh lime juice

1 teaspoon confectioners' sugar

2 to 3 ounces sparkling water

Lime wheel and 1 cranberry (or maraschino cherry), for garnish

Combine the rum, lime juice, and confectioners' sugar in a shaker, then add ice. Shake and strain into a chilled collins glass filled with ice and top off with sparkling water. To garnish, fold the lime wheel around the cranberry and skewer it. Then, rest the garnish on the edge of the glass.

Tom and Jerry

Think of this drink as a very adult eggnog—warm and luxurious, with a mix of spirits and spices. It starts with a sweet, custard-like batter to which brandy and rum are added, then the mixture is thickened with hot milk. We like to mix spirits here, but you can also make this just with brandy or just with rum. Prep the batter before the movie, then serve this drink when it arises—about two-thirds of the way through, when Baxter loans out his apartment to his boss on Christmas Eve. It makes a lovely dessert, presented as a tray of frothy mugs with a plate of sugar cookies. Note: This classic drink also appears in Giant *(page 134).*

SERVES 4 TO 6

For the batter

3 large eggs, separated

3 tablespoons confectioners' sugar

1 teaspoon vanilla extract

½ teaspoon ground cinnamon

For the cocktail

3 cups whole milk

4 ounces brandy

4 ounces gold rum

Freshly ground nutmeg, for garnish

For the batter, beat egg whites in a bowl until they form a stiff froth. In a separate bowl, beat the yolks well, then add sugar, vanilla, and cinnamon. Using a spatula, fold the whites into the yolk mixture and pop the batter into the fridge until you're ready to make cocktails—they should be made within several hours.

To make the hot drink, heat the milk on the stove in a saucepan and bring it to a simmer. Then remove the pan from the heat.

Fold the brandy and rum into the batter—use a spatula and stir just until mixed so that the batter remains fluffy.

Divide the batter between warmed mugs or tea cups. Whisk the hot milk into each cup—a fork works well. Grate nutmeg on top of each drink and serve.

Opposite: **Shirley MacLaine and Fred MacMurray, ringing in a new year**

Build-Your-Own Turkey and Cranberry Club Sandwiches

The triple-decker club sandwich is an American classic that has appeared on restaurant menus for more than a century, often with unique variations. Here, we add maple-roasted sweet potatoes in place of the extra bread layer, and we slather on cranberry chutney. While you can assemble these in advance for a viewing party (you can even use slider rolls), we love to invite people over for a build-your-own club night and ask everyone to bring a condiment. Pickles, mustards, chutneys, and flavored mayos or goat cheese spreads are all fair game.

SERVES 6 TO 8

1 loaf sandwich bread, thinly sliced and toasted

1 pack (16 ounces) thick-cut bacon, cooked

1 to 1½ pounds smoked turkey, sliced

6 to 8 crispy romaine lettuce leaves, washed and separated

Roasted Sweet Potato Coins (see page 154)

Cranberry sauce, jam, or chutney

Mayonnaise

To build a club sandwich, slather the toasted bread with condiments. Then add the fixings. Use the sweet potato coins as your middle layer.

Set the Scene ▰▰▰▰▰

Cue up some Johnny Mathis and prepare a round of Rum Collinses to serve with the mixed nuts and cheese crackers. We like to course this meal out, starting with drinks and snacks as the film begins, followed by a break in the middle to let everyone assemble their sandwiches. Then, we pop out to the kitchen and whisk together the Tom and Jerrys when they get mentioned. You can also present this meal as a throwback 1950s buffet; fill in around the edges with deviled eggs, veggies and dip, potato chips, slaw, and Jell-O. For fun decorating ideas inspired by this film, hang long wisps of tinsel from your tree, flank a typewriter with small poinsettias, and set out old playing cards to encourage a card game late into the evening.

"The tree is up and the Tom and Jerry mix is in the refrigerator." —C. C. BAXTER

Roasted Sweet Potato Coins

This makes enough for 6 to 8 sandwiches and is easily doubled.

2 large sweet potatoes, cut on the bias into ¼-inch coins

2 tablespoons extra-virgin olive oil

2 tablespoons maple syrup

1 teaspoon salt

Above: Jack Lemmon as C. C. Baxter, enjoying a chicken leg from a TV dinner

Preheat the oven to 400°F and line a pair of cookie sheets with parchment paper.

In a large bowl, toss the sweet potato rounds with olive oil, maple syrup, and salt. Divide the rounds between the two sheets, separating them so the potatoes don't overlap. Roast until browned on the edges, about 20 minutes, then remove the pans from the oven, and flip the rounds over. Roast another 10 minutes, until browned. Serve warm or at room temperature.

While You're Watching ...

★ Shirley MacLaine received her second Oscar nomination for Best Actress for her role in *The Apartment*. A Broadway Chorus girl turned actress, she leapt into stardom by playing the understudy in the 1957 musical *The Pajama Game*.

★ MacLaine's pixie haircut was a popular style in the 1950s, thanks to Audrey Hepburn, who sported a pixie-like no-fuss look in her debut film, *Roman Holiday* (page 119). The two actresses costarred in *The Children's Hour* (1961).

★ Watch for this: C. C. Baxter visits his boss with a bottle of nasal spray in his pocket—which he accidentally sprays into the air. Lemmon added this touch for comic relief (director Billy Wilder loved Lemmon's Chaplin-esque techniques). Cleverly, Lemmon filled the bottle with milk so that the spray would be visible on screen.

A rollicking office party

BREAKFAST AT TIFFANY'S (1961)

Menu

DIAMOND BRUNCH

Soyer au Champagne with Berries

Cardamom-Cinnamon Twists (with Coffee)

A TAXI ROLLS DOWN 5TH AVENUE AT 5 O'CLOCK IN THE MORNING and stops in front of Tiffany's. A passenger steps out, wearing a black evening gown with dark sunglasses. It's an iconic movie moment: She lingers in front of the store's diamond-lit windows and munches a pastry from a paper bag while sipping coffee from a paper cup. There you have it: breakfast at Tiffany's.

Based on the book by Truman Capote, this film tells the story of Holly Golightly (Audrey Hepburn), a wisp of a girl with childlike charm and an outsized sense of style. She hosts wild parties in her bare-bones apartment, stores her rotary telephone in a suitcase to muffle its ring, and calls her upstairs neighbor Paul Varjack (George Peppard) "Fred" because he reminds her of a long-lost brother. Determined to put her small-town upbringing behind her, Holly strives to make an impression on everyone she meets—and she always does, with her hats, her bouffant hairstyle, and her cigarette holder.

About halfway through the film, Paul invites Holly to spend the day together doing things they've never done before, like popping Champagne before breakfast and wandering through the vault-like public library. All the while, Holly mulls over her future engagement to one of the richest men in the world—trying to deny the chemistry bubbling between her and Paul. It's the story of two commitment-phobes falling in love.

Opposite: **Audrey Hepburn as Holly Golightly**

A must-see fashion movie loaded with exquisite Givenchy hats and dresses, *Breakfast at Tiffany's* manages to make tragic figures look magical and subsistence-living seem sumptuous. Break out a wine glass or pour yourself a glass of milk, or better yet—drop a scoop of ice cream into some Champagne.

Set the Scene ◄◄◄◄◄◄

Play some Henry Mancini as guests arrive, and if you have any old suitcases, consider stacking them for an impromptu coffee table—a DIY design cue from Holly's apartment. If you want to add a party favor, give each guest a box of Cracker Jack and a satin eye mask. They're both significant in the film. To round out this menu with other foods from the movie, you can add Martinis (page 41), an iceberg lettuce salad, and a cake with pink icing.

While You're Watching ...

★ You can't miss the opening song, "Moon River" by Henry Mancini, which establishes this film's doleful and dream-like feel. Mancini composed the song specifically for Hepburn's vocal range since she was not a trained singer. The song was almost cut by Paramount execs who wanted to shorten the film, but Hepburn insisted they keep it.

★ Mickey Rooney, one of the era's biggest male stars, plays Mr. Yunioshi, Holly's Japanese neighbor. His caricature-like role here has been heavily criticized; it's the only part of the film that doesn't wear well.

★ Marilyn Monroe had her eye on the role of Holly, but the producers thought Audrey Hepburn was the natural fit. Impossibly slender, she had a figure unlike other stars at the time, but her uncanny sense of fashion helped her choose costumes to boost her features, like capri pants with ballet flats.

Opposite: **Fashion first for Holly Golightly** | *Above:* **Hepburn and Peppard take a sip of whiskey**

"If I could find a real-life place that made me feel like Tiffany's . . . then I'd buy some furniture and give the cat a name."   —HOLLY GOLIGHTLY

Soyer au Champagne with Berries

Because milk and bubbles figure prominently in this movie, we like to serve this classic cocktail. It seems like the sort of drink Holly would have loved. We've tricked it out with berries to create a breakfast cocktail parfait, best eaten with a spoon. Serve it in a large martini glass or wine glass placed on a saucer, with berries strewn lazily across the top and around the stem. It should look absolutely decadent.

½ ounce brandy

½ ounce orange curaçao

½ ounce Luxardo Maraschino Liqueur

1 scoop vanilla ice cream or gelato

2 ounces Champagne, to top off

Freshly grated nutmeg, for garnish

Berries (raspberries, blueberries, strawberries, currants)

Shake brandy, orange curaçao, and Luxardo with ice and strain into a chilled cocktail glass over a scoop of ice cream. Top with Champagne and garnish with nutmeg and berries.

Serve with a spoon and straw, if desired.

Tip: To prep this drink before a party, simply batch the spirits, shake over ice, strain into a jar or pitcher, then refrigerate. Place your glasses in the freezer to chill. When guests arrive, set out the ice cream, glasses, and dishes of berries. Assemble them all at once, or let guests build their own.

Hepburn as the iconic Holly Golightly, with her pastry

Cardamom-Cinnamon Twists (with Coffee)

You know that pastry that Holly pulls from a white bakery bag during the first scene of the film? Well, we've studied it many times. Is it a cinnamon cruller? An apple fritter? Sure, you could pick up either at a bakery, but we decided to do something splendid and create a puff pastry twist, sprinkled with cinnamon, cardamom, and sparkly raw sugar. This recipe is a snap, and it will make your house smell gorgeous. We like to serve these twists in small white paper bags at the start of the film, alongside coffee.

SERVES 6 TO 8

1 sheet frozen puff pastry (half of a 17.3-ounce package), thawed

3 tablespoons unsalted butter, melted

2 teaspoons cinnamon

½ teaspoon ground cardamom

¼ cup raw sugar (or large-crystal sugar)

Preheat the oven to 400°F and line a baking sheet with parchment paper.

Unroll the pastry and brush it liberally with butter. In a small bowl, combine cinnamon, cardamom, and sugar. Sprinkle half of it over the pastry. Then use a rolling pin to roll the pastry thinner and sprinkle again.

Using a pizza cutter, slice the pastry in half. Then cut each half into even 1-inch strips. Twist the strips and place them onto the baking sheet. Bake for 15 to 20 minutes, or until lightly browned. Serve warm.

Holly talks to a mysterious party guest (Michael Quinlivan), with an eye patch.

BLUE HAWAII (1961)

Menu

DINNER ON THE BEACH

Mai Tai

Coconut Fish Curry

Pineapple Sundaes

B LUE WATER, COCONUT PALMS, AND HAWAIIAN GUITARS MAKE A vibrant backdrop for a beachy evening of cocktails. Never mind that the acting here can be a little stiff; the point of this musical romp is style over substance. It is, after all, a surf movie. Whatever it may lack, it does not short viewers on The King. You certainly get your fill of Elvis, who, at a trim twenty-six, was just out of the army and ready to make female audiences swoon. And sing along. The soundtrack to *Blue Hawaii* spent 79 weeks on the Billboard chart, 20 of them at #1.

The plot is sitcom simple: Young Chad Gates (Elvis) is a returning soldier who is keen to get out of his uniform and back into his swim trunks so he can hit the beach with his girlfriend. While his dad wants him to take a position at the family pineapple plant, Chad has other ambitions. He signs up to work as a tour guide. From there, it's all crooning and convertibles with lots of ladies bouncing around beside him. Look out for Chad's mother, Sarah Lee Gates (Angela Lansbury of *Murder, She Wrote*) in a delightfully humorous role. Lansbury was barely ten years older than Elvis! What a trip to watch her play a southern hostess, always perfectly appointed, with cocktail in hand.

Opposite: **Abigail Prentice and Elvis on the beach**

Mai Tai

Perhaps the quintessential drink of the Hawaiian Islands, this 1940s invention is classically tiki, which means layered rums, complex flavor, and exotic syrups and spirits. Don't let that scare you! A true Mai Tai is a revelation, nothing like the sticky-sweet umbrella drinks that have become approximations of these recipes at many hotel bars. Make a batch of homemade orgeat (pronounced OR-jzah)—an ambrosial almond syrup—or look for prepared orgeat online, and fix yourself Mai Tais all week long. They appear over and over in Blue Hawaii, *and with good reason: If Elvis is the King of Rock 'n' Roll, the Mai Tai is Queen of Island Drinks.*

1 ounce dark rum

1 ounce amber rum (rhum agricole, such as Clément)

½ ounce orange curaçao

1 ounce fresh lime juice

¼ ounce orgeat (see below)

Mint sprig, for garnish

Lime wheel, for garnish

Shake ingredients with ice and strain into a rocks glass or hurricane glass with ice. Garnish with mint and lime.

"Chadwick's a growing boy, I don't think it's appropriate of you to give him intoxicating libations." —SARAH LEE GATES

Orgeat

½ cup Demerara sugar

Peel of half a grapefruit

1 scant cup almond milk (preferably Silk Original)

8 drops almond extract

4 drops orange flower water

In a small mixing bowl, add sugar and grapefruit peels. Stir, then let grapefruit peels sit for one hour, so that the oil from the peel seeps into the crystals. After an hour, add almond milk to the sugar mixture and remove the peel (chopsticks work well). Add almond extract and orange flower water. Stir well or shake the mixture in a jar. It will take several minutes for the sugar to incorporate. Once combined, cover and refrigerate (it will thicken into a syrup). Orgeat will keep for about 1 week.

Coconut Fish Curry (PHOTO ON PAGE 166)

We like to channel Hawaiian 1960s cookery with this easy curry. It's creamy and mild so you can taste the fish, and the toppings—bananas, cashews, green onions—really give it dimension. Scale it up or down, depending on the size of your dinner party, and feel free to mix in shrimp or vegetables (red and green bell peppers are especially good). The flavors in this dish get better with time, so you can make this sauce in advance and add the fish later. Serve over rice or mashed root vegetables. Note: You can make this dish with fresh or frozen fish. Frozen fish gives off a little more water, so you may want to dial back the broth and add it later, if needed.

SERVES 4 TO 6

2 tablespoons unsalted butter

3 small garlic cloves, minced

1½ tablespoons finely chopped or grated fresh ginger

1 medium onion, diced

1 bay leaf

2 tablespoons curry powder (we like Penzeys Sweet Curry powder)

2 tablespoons all-purpose white flour

1 can (13½ ounces) coconut milk

¼ cup broth (chicken or vegetable)

1 teaspoon salt

1 pound to 1½ pounds fresh fish (mahi mahi or tilapia), cut into 2-inch pieces

½ cup chopped cashews, for garnish

4 green onions, sliced, for garnish

2 bananas, sliced, for garnish

Melt butter in a medium-size pot or Dutch oven over medium heat. Add garlic cloves, ginger, onion, and bay leaf. Cook until the onion is translucent but not browned, about 5 minutes. Add curry powder and flour, then slowly whisk in coconut milk and broth.

Simmer on low heat, stirring occasionally, until the mixture thickens, about 20 minutes. Season with salt, and taste for balance.

Add fish pieces and cover. Simmer just until the fish is cooked through, about 4 minutes. Remove bay leaf, and serve with garnishes.

Pineapple Sundaes

Cube fresh pineapple, divide the cubes up between bowls, and top each one with a generous scoop of vanilla ice cream or frozen yogurt. Add warm chocolate sauce and toasted slivered almonds. For added decadence, soak the pineapple in rum before serving.

Elvis serenading with his ukulele

Set the Scene ▄▄▄▄▄

Cue the soundtrack, hire the Elvis impersonator, and put up the cabana! It's time to get tiki-comfortable for this backdrop to your Pacific island getaway. Since this meal is all about the garnish, we like to set up a Mai Tai bar with a variety of sliced fruit and long bamboo skewers, then invite friends to build their own drinks with wild plumage. Pineapple wedges, citrus moons, melon slivers, cherries, and berries all work well. You can even hold a "best garnish" contest. At prime tiki bars, it's popular to carve lime rinds and create fruit origami, like banana dolphins—just Google "tiki garnishes" for ideas. For a party centerpiece, scatter shells around an orchid or sago palm. Dress in Hawaiian prints and white slacks, and for a starter, serve Spicy Popcorn (page 60) or a crunchy snack mix with dried pineapple.

While You're Watching...

★ If you turn up the sound as Elvis first disembarks from the plane, you can hear the hundreds of fans screaming as they watched the shoot.

★ The red MG roadster from the opening scene of this movie is on display at Graceland.

Right: **Elvis singing on the beach**

DR. NO [1962]

Menu

A SPY PARTY

Vesper Martini (and Red Stripe Beer)

Jerk Shrimp Skewers

Oven-Roasted Plantains and
Mango Dipping Sauce

UNLIKE MODERN JAMES BOND FILMS, *Dr. No* was shot on a relatively low budget. Nevertheless, it establishes the formula for all the later 007 movies—a dashing British spy (Sean Connery), exotic sets (Jamaica), the hot "Bond girl" (Ursula Andress), and a shadowy evil genius bent on world destruction. The car chases and the suspenseful—and inventive—ways to eliminate Bond are just part of the fun ride.

The first James Bond movie touched off an international sensation, not only for 007 and his penchant for double entendre, but also for his spirit of choice, vodka. After *Dr. No*, vodka sales soared in the United States, becoming over time the number-one-selling liquor. Suddenly, shaken martinis were the rage.

The suave and sophisticated Bond action hero has clearly been a hit with subsequent generations, and the films are now the longest-running franchise in movie history—50 years and counting. The new movies may be filled with more gadgets and more budget-busting action sequences than the original *Dr. No*, but audiences will still thrill at the first use of that signature opening theme over the credits, delivered so often while surrounded by glamorous cocktails, couture dresses, and guns: "Bond . . . James Bond."

Above: **Andress in a now-legendary swimsuit** | *Opposite:* **Bond . . . James Bond**

Vesper Martini (PHOTO ON PAGE 176–177)

James Bond liked his drink "large and very strong and very cold and very well made," or so he says in Ian Fleming's Casino Royale, *published in 1953. The drink is so named because vespers are the traditional sunset evening prayer, known as the "violet hour," a.k.a. Martini time. The original recipe called for Gordon's gin and vodka, plus half a measure of Kina Lillet. There are some updates in order to achieve this recipe today: Kina Lillet is no longer available, and the closest replacement is Cocchi Americano. The Gordon's gin formula has also changed, so to achieve the original 94-proof taste, use either Tanqueray or Brokers. This drink is properly stirred since it does not contain citrus or egg—one of the golden rules of bartending (page 9)—but go ahead and shake it if you must.*

---

3 ounces gin

1 ounce vodka

¼ ounce Cocchi Americano

Lemon twist, for garnish

Stir or shake ingredients with ice and strain into a chilled martini glass. Twist the lemon peel over the drink to express some of the oil, then slide the peel into the glass.

While You're Watching...

★ Dr. No's magnified fish are the result of the studio not being able to find the right film clip. Rather than continue hunting for a proper background, they simply had Dr. No explain the windows were magnifying.

★ Sorry ladies, Sean Connery wore a toupée in the *Bond* films—and already was wearing one here.

★ To get a suitable—and signature—feel for his suits, director Terence Young asked Connery to sleep in them.

Ursula Andress and Sean Connery

Jerk Shrimp Skewers (PHOTO ON PAGE 176–177)

Serve these spicy skewers as an appetizer or on a bed of fluffy rice with a drizzle of the spicy dipping sauce (page 179). This marinade is one of our favorites for the summer grill. It's hot, but not killer. A cold lager (Red Stripe) is a perfect accompaniment.

SERVES 4 TO 6

1 medium white onion, chopped

3 medium green onions, chopped

2 Scotch Bonnet chiles, seeded and chopped

4 medium garlic cloves

1 tablespoon Chinese five spice powder

1 tablespoon ground allspice berries

1 tablespoon freshly ground black pepper

1 teaspoon dried thyme

1 teaspoon freshly grated nutmeg

1 teaspoon salt

3 tablespoons fresh lime juice

1 teaspoon distilled white vinegar

1 bay leaf

3 tablespoons soy sauce

1 tablespoon vegetable oil

2 pounds peeled, uncooked large or jumbo shrimp

In a food processor, combine white onion, green onions, chiles, garlic, five spice powder, allspice, pepper, thyme, nutmeg, salt, lime juice, vinegar, and bay leaf. With the machine still running, add soy sauce and oil.

Toss the shrimp in the jerk marinade. Cover and refrigerate for 2 to 3 hours.

Skewer the shrimp, and grill for 2 to 3 minutes per side, or broil 2 minutes per side on a foil-lined baking sheet.

Set the Scene ◄◄◄◄◄◄

While James Bond spends most of his time in relaxed Caribbean garb in this film, it's hard to get away from the image of the suit or tuxedo. Feel free to glam it up with an eye toward the casino and country club set, or just take it easy and go beachy. Whichever you prefer, cue the steel drum band and enjoy the food. The vibe should be sexy and subdued.

"One medium-dry Vodka martini.
Mixed like you said, sir, but not stirred." —WAITER

Oven Roasted Plantains with Mango Dipping Sauce (PHOTO ON PAGE 176–177)

These thin plantain chips taste best made with coconut oil, though you can also use olive oil. Use the dipping sauce for the shrimp, too. It's easily doubled.

For the plantains

2 green plantains

2 tablespoons coconut oil, melted

1 teaspoon garlic salt

½ teaspoon freshly ground black pepper

For the dipping sauce

2 tablespoons prepared mango chutney

1 tablespoon apple cider vinegar

½ cup plain yogurt

¼ teaspoon hot sauce (or to taste)

1 teaspoon chopped cilantro, for garnish

Preheat the oven to 400°F and line a pair of baking pans with parchment paper.

Peel the plantains—the skin will be tough, so use a paring knife to chop off the ends, then score the sides lengthwise as you would an orange. Remove the peel carefully, using the knife.

Slice the plantains into thin coins, the thinner, the better. Toss the coins with oil, then sprinkle with salt and pepper.

Spread the plantains onto the baking sheets, making sure they don't overlap. Bake for 15 to 20 minutes or until the edges brown. You may want to flip them halfway through baking, if they brown too quickly.

For the dipping sauce: Combine the chutney and vinegar in a small bowl. Stir in the yogurt and add hot sauce to taste. Garnish with cilantro. For a smooth dipping sauce, puree in a blender or small food processor.

Opposite: **Actress Eunice Grayson putting in Bond's apartment**

THE GRADUATE (1967)

Menu

SWINGIN' CALIFORNIA POOL PARTY

Pimm's Popsicles

Teriyaki Salmon Bowls

STYLISHLY FILMED, with a soundtrack by Simon & Garfunkel, *The Graduate* follows young Benjamin Braddock (Dustin Hoffman) as he lounges around the pool instead of selecting grad schools—and begins an affair with the much older wife of his father's business partner, Mrs. Robinson (Anne Bancroft). A coming-of-age story that captures the zeitgeist of the late 1960s, *The Graduate* is full of ennui and disillusionment, mixed with modern design and California architecture. It's the sort of movie that makes you want to climb aboard a rubber raft with a boozy Popsicle (see page 184) and forget all cares.

Cinematically, *The Graduate* is a fascinating example of "anti-Hollywood" style influenced by French New Wave films of the time, such as Jean-Luc Godard's *Breathless* (1960) and François Truffaut's *Jules and Jim* (1962). Shots are held overly long, and the story unfolds without directorial comment to create a kind of pervasive neutrality. As you witness a blank-faced Benjamin attempt to navigate the now-alien world of his upper-crust Cali parents, you can't help but feel the quakes of this era's deep generation gap.

Complex and quietly dramatic, this sophomore effort of director Mike Nichols (*Who's Afraid of Virginia Woolf?*, *Silkwood*) burns brightly as a quintessential American film about late 1960s mainstream youth culture.

Opposite: **Dustin Hoffman and Anne Bancroft**

While You're Watching...

★ The attendant at the hotel where Ben meets Mrs. Robinson is Buck Henry, the film's screenwriter. He was also a regular host on *Saturday Night Live*.

★ Watch for the animal-print wardrobe that Mrs. Robinson wears whenever she's on the prowl and the ever-present aquatic imagery that surrounds Ben.

Set the Scene ◄◄◄◄◄◄

Let the word "Plastics" influence your choice in table setting (think Bakelite candlesticks). Sixties suburban home design plays a huge role here: Mid-century Modern furniture, shag rugs, home wet bars, decorative ashtrays, not to mention characters dressed in leisure wear with giant sunglasses. Wheel in your potted palm, your fish tank. Or, break out your snorkel and flippers to re-create the film's epic pool party scene. If you fire up the grill for the salmon, mix some easy summer drinks, like a Rum Collins (page 150) or a Daiquiri (page 99).

Opposite: **Dustin Hoffman in the pool** | *Above:* **Ben's graduation party**

Pimm's Popsicles

The classic British cocktail, the Pimm's Cup, might be the perfect poolside drink. Related to Sangria, it features fresh fruit, ginger beer, herbaceous Pimm's No. 1, and mint. But perhaps one better is Pimm's in frozen Popsicle form! All you need are twelve 3-ounce ice-pop molds, and you've got cocktails on sticks. Freeze these the night before a party for a novel way to cool down and imbibe in style.

SERVES 12

1¼ cups Pimm's No. 1

½ cup fresh lemon juice

2 ounces fresh lime juice

1 bottle (12 ounces) ginger beer, flat

½ cup water

Strawberries, hulled and sliced

Cucumber, thinly sliced

Fresh mint leaves

Combine Pimm's, lemon and lime juice, ginger beer, and water. Place a few slices of strawberries and cucumbers along with a sprig of mint down into each Popsicle mold. Pour in Pimm's mixture, insert sticks, and freeze.

"For god's sake, Mrs. Robinson. Here we are. You got me into your house. You give me a drink. You . . . put on music. Now you start opening up your personal life to me and tell me your husband won't be home for hours . . ." —BENJAMIN BRADDOCK

Teriyaki Salmon Bowls

The Graduate is full of fish tanks, pool parties, and aquatic imagery—we play off it here with a fish bowl that borrows from California cuisine. Light and fresh, this meal is a cinch to prep the night before or the morning of a party. The salmon is best marinated all day, though we've definitely thrown this together in an evening. Searing the salmon, then finishing it in the oven, yields a gloriously caramelized piece of fish that remains moist and flaky inside.

SERVES 4

3 tablespoons apple cider vinegar

1 tablespoon corn starch

½ cup soy sauce

½ cup brown sugar, packed

3-inch thumb of ginger, peeled and chopped (about 2 tablespoons)

4 garlic cloves, chopped

3 tablespoons honey

2 (5-ounce) salmon fillets, 1 inch thick

3 cups steamed brown rice

1 carrot, shredded

1 cup steamed and shelled edamame

1 small head broccoli, chopped and steamed

1 cup sunflower sprouts (or other sprouts), for garnish

3 teaspoons toasted sesame seeds, for garnish

In a blender, combine vinegar, corn starch, soy sauce, sugar, ginger, garlic, and honey. Pour the marinade into a large resealable plastic bag and add the salmon. Refrigerate for 8 to 12 hours, turning occasionally to coat the fish.

To cook the salmon, preheat the oven to 425°F.

Heat a medium-size skillet or nonstick pan on medium-high until a drop of water sizzles. Add the salmon (reserve the marinade) skin-side up and sear for 2 to 3 minutes, or until the underside browns. Then, slide the skillet into the oven—don't flip the salmon—or, if your pan isn't oven-safe, just slide the fish onto a foil-lined baking sheet and pop it into the oven to finish. It should cook in approximately 6 minutes, unless it's very thin. The salmon is done when the meat flakes (use a fork to test).

While the fish is cooking, heat the marinade in a small saucepan over medium heat. It will thicken in less than a minute.

Remove the salmon from the oven, and cut it into four equal parts.

To assemble the bowls: Divide the rice between four dishes and drizzle each one with some sauce. Then, top with salmon, carrot, edamame, broccoli, and sprouts. Finish with sesame seeds.

Tip: Start your brown rice about 30 minutes before you preheat the oven to cook the salmon. Steam your edamame after you put the fish into the oven.

Above: **Katharine Ross, who plays Mrs. Robinson's daughter, and Hoffman**

FUNNY GIRL (1968)

Menu

BEFORE BROADWAY PATÉ BOARD

Bijou Cocktail

Chicken Liver Paté with
the Works

THE MOVIE THAT LAUNCHED BARBRA STREISAND'S ACTING CAREER ends with one of the funniest seduction scenes involving food. When Park Avenue playboy Nick Arnstein (Omar Sharif) offers showgirl Fanny Brice (Streisand) paté, she thinks it's a liquid—and is surprised to realize it's just "chopped liver." Streisand plays a girl from humble means (her parents own a saloon on the Lower East Side) who makes it big on the New York stage as part of the Broadway spectacular the Ziegfeld Follies. Proving that brains can outshine beauty, she embellishes her acts with clever improvisation and turns herself into a comic star.

Based on the real story of Fanny Brice, the popular comedienne of the 1920s and '30s, *Funny Girl* pops with Technicolor costumes, delectably garish sets, and sparkling show tunes. The film originated on Broadway, then made its way to the screen, propelling Streisand into diva-dom. Her abilities as a singer and comedic actress earned her an Academy Award and paved the way for a six-decade career gilded with Grammys, Emmys, Oscars, and Tonys.

Invite your best Broadway-loving friends over for a bash, and when you answer the door, say, "Hello, gorgeous."

Opposite: **Omar Sharif and Barbra Streisand**

Bijou Cocktail (PHOTO ON PAGES 192–193)

Funny Girl features a number of drink scenes, most notably an emerald green Mint Frappé—straight green crème de menthe poured over shaved ice. But who wants to drink straight crème de menthe? For a green drink that will turn heads, and pair with paté, why not reach for something more classic, like a Bijou? Made with gin and Chartreuse—a French liqueur the color of peridot—the Bijou is stunning. Its name, which means "jewel" in French, couldn't be more perfect for a movie that rocks the sparkle.

1½ ounces gin

¾ ounce green Chartreuse

1 ounce blanc vermouth (like Dolin Blanc)

2 dashes orange bitters

Stir ingredients with ice and strain into a chilled martini glass.

Above: **A bejeweled Fanny Brice (Streisand)**

Chicken Liver Paté with the Works (PHOTO ON PAGES 192–193)

Funny Girl made paté a star—it was served on opening night at a party on the grounds of the Astor Hotel and became inextricably linked with both the film and the Broadway production. Not a paté fan? This version is so velvety, it will win you over. Paté heads, you're going to go crazy! Quality Madeira is key here; we like to use a Historic Series Madeira from Rare Wine Co. such as their Charleston Sercial. You can serve glasses of it alongside your paté board, in addition to cocktails and Champagne.

For the works: We like to serve this paté on a large wooden board or platter, surrounded by heaps of crostini, bagel chips, chopped egg, minced red onion, capers, lox, cream cheese, chives, and an assortment of pickles.

SERVES 4 TO 6

8 tablespoons butter, divided

1 shallot, finely chopped (about ⅛ cup)

1 teaspoon fresh chopped thyme

12 ounces chicken livers, cut into 1-inch pieces

⅓ cup Madeira

⅓ cup heavy whipping cream

½ teaspoon salt

1 allspice berry, ground (scant ¼ teaspoon)

Melt two tablespoons of butter in a saucepan over medium-high heat. Add the shallot and thyme, and sauté until sweated but not browned. Add the chicken livers and sauté until lightly cooked. They should be lightly browned on the outside but still a bit pink inside. Transfer the mixture to a food processor.

Add Madeira to the pan and cook on medium-high heat until it has reduced by half. Then, add it to the food processor, along with the cream, 6 tablespoons butter, salt, and allspice. Process until smooth.

Pass the mixture through a sieve into a serving dish—this will make for a truly velvety spread (read: without grittiness). Cover tightly and place in the refrigerator to set. Chill before serving.

"A bit of paté?"—NICK ARNSTEIN

"I drink it all day."—FANNY BRICE

Set the Scene ▰▰▰▰▰

Break out your most over-the-top table settings and your wildest club attire—*Funny Girl* is all about outrageous fashion, thanks to Irene Sharaff, who won five Academy Awards for her costume design over the years of her long career. During Fanny Brice's seduction scene, Nick Arnstein pulls out all the stops with yellow roses, glowing candelabras, and a table for two decked out with gold and copper accents. He also gifts her a blue marble egg. We like to serve our paté board on a red velvet backdrop.

While You're Watching ...

★ The onscreen romance was happening in real life as well. Streisand and Sharif had an affair during the shooting of the film, which contributed to the end of her marriage to Elliott Gould.

★ Producer Ray Stark was the son-in-law of the real Fanny Brice.

★ "My Man," the final number, was performed live rather than lip-synced.

Opposite: **Streisand as Fanny Brice** | *Above:* **Omar Sharif and Barbra Streisand on set**

THE STING (1973)

Menu
MOBSTER NIGHT

Old Fashioned

Chicago-Style Deep Dish Pizza

B AR FIGHTS, BURLESQUE DANCERS, BACKROOM GAMBLING, and counterfeit money all find their way into this Depression-era grifter movie starring Paul Newman and Robert Redford. The two reunited after *Butch Cassidy and the Sundance Kid* (1969) to star in this film about a pair of 1930s con men. Beloved for its ragtime score and retro lens set on the city of Chicago, *The Sting* uses muted colors and classic 1930s style—thanks to costume designer Edith Head—to resurrect the Windy City's gangster culture. To be clear, this film is also loved for its handsome-devil duo: Newman and Redford never looked better.

With a terrific script and a great soundtrack full of Scott Joplin tunes, *The Sting* offers a rollicking thrill ride aboard trains and antique cars. There's loads of hooch to boot, particularly bourbon and gin. What could be a more appropriate cocktail to serve alongside it than the Old Fashioned, a rogue concoction that became America's first cocktail?

Opposite: **Robert Redford and Paul Newman**

Old Fashioned

In the Midwest, the Old Fashioned is typically made with brandy—legend has it that the Korbel brothers kicked off this trend at the 1893 Chicago World's Fair. In Midwestern bars it's common to muddle an orange wheel and a cherry in the bottom of the glass, add bitters and brandy, then top the drink off with a hit of 7-Up. The very thought makes cocktail purists shiver. Below, you'll find a traditional Old Fashioned recipe. This is the drink that launched the American cocktail as a phenomenon—a drink prepared for an individual, not for a group (i.e., a punch). One of the earliest references (1880) appears in the Chicago Tribune when presidential candidate Samuel Tilden called for a toast.

1 sugar cube

2 to 3 dashes Angostura bitters

2 ounces whiskey or brandy

1 teaspoon water

Orange peel, for garnish

Place the sugar cube in a chilled rocks glass. Dash in the bitters and muddle, coating the bottom and the sides of the glass. Drop in a large cube of ice, then add the spirit of your choice and water. Stir. To garnish, twist the peel over the surface of the cocktail to express the oil, and drop the peel into the drink.

Redford and Newman cast their chips as gamblers

Chicago-Style Deep Dish Pizza

Baked in an iron skillet, this thick-crusted pie can be filled with any of your favorite toppings. There's just one catch: The toppings should be placed in the middle of a Chicago-style pizza, sandwiched between gooey cheese on the bottom and red sauce on the top. This brilliant inversion prevents the crust from getting soggy, and it allows the liquid in the sauce to evaporate, making for deeply concentrated tomato flavor. Ah-mazing. If you need a nibble while this is baking, serve a round of wedge salads or a dish of salted nuts with a relish tray of carrots, celery, radishes, and dill pickles—a staple at Midwestern supper clubs, once the dinnertime haunt of Old-Fashioned-guzzling mobsters. We like to use Mark Bittman's basic pizza dough recipe from The Essential New York Times Cookbook, which makes enough to fill a 12-inch cast-iron skillet with some dough left over to make a second small pizza.

SERVES 4

For the dough

2½ to 3 cups all-purpose white flour

2 teaspoons active dry yeast (1 packet)

2 teaspoons salt

1 cup warm (wrist-temperature) water

2 tablespoons extra-virgin olive oil

For the sauce

1 can (14½-ounce) chopped tomatoes, drained

2 tablespoons tomato paste

1 tablespoon brown sugar

1 teaspoon balsamic vinegar

3 large garlic cloves

½ teaspoon red pepper flakes

½ teaspoon dried basil

½ teaspoon dried oregano

1 teaspoon salt

For the toppings

2 tablespoons extra-virgin olive oil

1 8-ounce ball fresh mozzarella, sliced

8 ounces mushrooms, sliced and sautéed

1 red onion, sliced and sautéed

1 green bell pepper, roughly chopped and sautéed

5 to 7 ounces pepperoni or Canadian bacon, sliced

6 to 8 large green or black olives, sliced

1 cup freshly grated Parmigiano Reggiano

To make the dough: Set out a large bowl and combine half the flour, the yeast, and the salt. Stir. Pour in the liquids. Stir until smooth, then slowly begin adding flour, about ¼ cup at a time. When the dough gets too thick to stir, flour your hands and transfer the dough to a clean work surface that you have generously sprinkled with

"Luther said I could learn from you. I already know how to drink." —JOHNNY HOOKER

flour. Plan to knead the dough for about 10 minutes, incorporating flour as needed. Don't worry about using the entire 3 cups of flour; your goal is to generate an elastic dough using as little extra flour as possible—usually 2½ cups flour is just right.

Transfer the dough to a bowl and cover with plastic wrap. It should be about the size of a grapefruit. Set it in a warm spot to double in size, about 1 to 2 hours. (Placing it in an oven set to 100°F works perfectly.)

Return the dough to your floured surface. Shape two-thirds of it into a large ball (this will be your deep-dish pizza crust) and the rest into a small ball (this can be a mini deep-dish pizza). Dust them with flour and cover them with a towel. Let them rise for another 20 minutes.

To make the sauce: Drop all of the sauce ingredients into a blender and pulse until well combined.

To assemble the pizza: Preheat the oven to 450°F.

In a 12-inch cast-iron skillet, drizzle 2 tablespoons of olive oil and grease the entire pan well with your fingertips.

With oiled fingers, press the large ball of pizza dough into the skillet, pushing it an inch or so up the sides.

Layer the mozzarella slices along the bottom of the dough. Add your remaining toppings. Spoon the sauce over the top, then sprinkle on the Parmigiano Reggiano.

Bake for 25 to 30 minutes, then let rest for 5 to 10 minutes before serving.

Above: **Paul Newman and Robert Redford** | *Opposite:* **Robert Redford**

Set the Scene ◄◄◄◄◄

Reach for your dice and your bottles of bourbon. Much of this movie is shot in back rooms or warehouses, so keep the lights low and set out a couple of ashtrays. You won't find much food in this film, although Johnny Hooker (Robert Redford) orders a supper of meatloaf, apple pie, and a cup of coffee shortly before getting caught. If you want to create some vibe, serve this menu on newsprint (see note below) and don't fuss over the details, except for your suspenders and pinky rings.

While You're Watching...

★ Director George Roy Hill, who received an Academy Award for *The Sting*, combed back issues of *The Saturday Evening Post* to gain inspiration about the period. Notice how the film incorporates newspaper images from the 1930s between major scenes.

★ Robert Shaw's limp wasn't faked. He slipped and fell on a handball court before filming began, and his injury became part of his role as Doyle Lonnegan.

★ The diner scenes were shot on the backlot at Universal Studios. The set was also used for the diner scenes in *Back to the Future* (1985).

AMERICAN GRAFFITI [1973]

Menu

A NIGHT AT THE DRIVE-IN

Boozy Shake

Classic Cheeseburgers

Diner Coffee (suggested)

THE FILM GEORGE LUCAS MADE BEFORE *STAR WARS*—yes, that's right!— *American Graffiti* is loaded with 1950s nostalgia and young stars before they were known: Ron Howard, Richard Dreyfuss, Harrison Ford, Mackenzie Phillips, Cindy Williams, and a blink-and-you'll miss it cameo by Suzanne Somers. Based on Lucas's boyhood experiences cruising around Modesto, California, the script for this film was turned down by every major studio—only to become the sleeper hit of the decade, thanks to a little help from producer and friend Francis Ford Coppola. The movie also went on to inspire the popular television sitcom *Happy Days*, with its story of small-town life, launching the television careers of many of its stars.

In *American Graffiti*, Mel's drive-in serves as the high-school hangout for guys who love cruising and girls whose strongest curse word is "rats!" In other words, car-centric nostalgia served alongside Cherry Cokes. The premise is simple: Friends Curt Henderson (Richard Dreyfuss) and Steve Bolander (Ron Howard) are cruising around on their last night before going off to college. That's enough time for relationships to flounder and flourish, for drinking games to begin, and for white-walled tires to spin. The soundtrack is a veritable jukebox sampler from the 1950s and '60s, and the hairdos are slicked and splendid. What could be better than grilling some burgers, putting your arm around your best girl, and sharing a Boozy Shake on the couch?

Boozy Shake

A classic vanilla milkshake is just the accompaniment to this film, so much of which takes place outside the classic diner. We like to add a little additional zing with either vanilla vodka or Kringle Cream liqueur, which tastes exactly like a frosted Danish pastry. Sure, the recipe is not low-cal, but once you try this surpassingly creamy, decadent combination you'll give yourself a pass on movie night.

SERVES 1 TO 2

2 cups vanilla ice cream

¼ cup heavy whipping cream

½ cup (4 ounces) Kringle Cream liqueur or vanilla vodka

1 tablespoon sugar

½ teaspoon vanilla extract

Combine ingredients in a blender and pulse until smooth. Serve in a tall, chilled glass with a straw.

Candy Clark, Charles Martin Smith, and Ron Howard

"Look, creep. You want a
knuckle sandwich?" —VIC

"Uh, no thanks. I'm waiting for
a double Chucky Chuck." —TERRY

Classic Cheeseburgers (PHOTO ON PAGE 207)

At Mel's drive-in, waitresses deliver dinner trays on roller skates, and the fare is classic Americana: burgers, shakes, and fries. Our recipe features a few great tricks for making juicy, memorable burgers every time. Just be sure to get good-quality sesame or potato buns.

SERVES 4

1 pound ground beef, preferably 80 percent lean

2 tablespoons butter, divided

4 hamburger buns

Salt and freshly ground black pepper

4 slices American cheese

Burger toppings: sliced tomatoes, sliced onions, lettuce, ketchup, mustard, pickles

Handling the beef as little as possible, divide it into four equal parts and press into patties slightly larger than the burger buns. Using your thumb, make a shallow dimple in the top of each patty (this chef trick prevents the patties from shrinking when they cook).

Heat a skillet over medium heat and add 1 tablespoon of butter. Toast buns on both sides, and set aside.

Turn your stove to medium-high heat, melt another tablespoon of butter, and then add the burger patties. Season the burgers with pepper and salt, and let them sear for 3 to 5 minutes. Flip the burgers. If there is not a dark sear on the underside, increase the heat. Season again with salt and pepper. If you're melting the cheese, place slices on top of the burger now. Cook 3 to 5 minutes. Do not overcook. There should be a little visible pinkness for medium-rare. Transfer burgers to toasted buns and add toppings.

Opposite: **Drag racers on Main Street**

Set the Scene ◄◄◄◄◄

Rev your engines, it's time for some classic American road cuisine. A few diner-centric props go a long way—trays for the food, red diner baskets, wax paper to wrap the burgers, and 1950s jukebox hits. Better yet, find the film's soundtrack. Anything from preppy clothes to leather jackets works well here, if you want to dress the part. Don't forget to roll up a pack of cigarettes in your sleeve. This movie night is perfect for a family reunion or for those who adore classic cars.

While You're Watching…

★ The license plate on character John Milner's car is THX-138, a reference to George Lucas's first feature film, *THX-1138* (also produced by Francis Ford Coppola).

★ The defunct Mel's Drive-in was reopened to shoot the movie, and it was then demolished after the filming was complete.

★ George Lucas was inspired by Federico Fellini's *I Vitelloni*, the story of five friends coming of age.

ROCKY (1976)

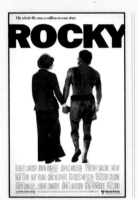

Menu
SOUTH PHILLY SUPPER

The Philadelphia Special

Italian Stallion Hoagie

Chocolate Turtles (suggested)

WRITTEN BY FILM STAR SYLVESTER STALLONE, *Rocky* is the story of heavyweight boxer Rocky Balboa, who trains in a Philadelphia meat cooler where his friend Pauly works as a butcher. With its young cast and working-class subject matter, few movie execs expected this to become a phenomenon, but it went on to rate as the highest-grossing movie of its time, after *Star Wars*. Rocky's depiction of an underdog from the gritty streets of south Philadelphia has, by now, become iconic. Every tourist who visits Philadelphia knows to run up the "Rocky steps" leading to the city's majestic art museum, which appears during his training regime.

The story opens around Thanksgiving and features a turkey flung from the oven into a back alley, but the film's real culinary soul appears in passing, as *Rocky* moves through the city's row-house-lined streets, skirting corner stores framed by advertisements for cold cuts. What better cuisine to highlight in this red-meat-centric movie than an Italian hoagie, lined with cured meats and drizzled with vinegar and olive oil. In Philadelphia, the hoagie (known in other regions as a "grinder" or "sub sandwich") is a specialty of many sandwich shops, including Sarcone's in South Philly, which has perfected the hoagie roll—an airy bun with a shatter-thin crust.

Grab your red satin robe, wrap a towel around your neck, and prepare for a winning evening.

Opposite: **Sylvester Stallone as Rocky Balboa**

"You're gonna eat lightnin' and you're gonna crap thunder!" —MICKEY

The Philadelphia Special

In the City of Brotherly Love, a pounder of PBR and a shot of whiskey has been a longstanding tra-dition. To locals, it also goes by the term "citywide" or "happy meal." Whatever you call it, the com-bination makes for quick and dirty drinkin' at its finest. In Rocky, you'll see Four Roses Bourbon.

1 shot whiskey

1 can Pabst Blue Ribbon

Shoot back the whiskey. Nurse the beer.

Italian Stallion Hoagie

Modeled after the award-winning Italian hoagie sold at Paesano's in Kensington, the Philadel-phia neighborhood where Rocky was filmed, this sandwich includes a trifecta of beautifully spiced traditional Italian meats. We like to build a single mastodon of a sandwich, then let people slice off as much as they dare. You can also invite people over to build their own hoa-gies. Seek out the best cured meats and sharp Provolone you can find from an Italian specialty foods shop, and be sure to grab some pickles and chips.

SERVES 6

6 hoagie rolls

½ pound aged Provolone, sliced

½ pound hot coppa (spicy cured pork shoulder), thinly sliced

½ pound mortadella, thinly sliced

½ pound Genoa salami, thinly sliced

1 small white onion, thinly shaved into circles

3 large Roma tomatoes, thinly sliced

Several handfuls arugula

Extra-virgin olive oil

Red wine vinegar

Sweet pickled peppers, for garnish

Hot pickled peppers, for garnish

Dried oregano, for garnish

Salt and freshly ground black pepper, to taste

Slice the hoagie rolls lengthwise, without cutting all the way through. Traditional-ists usually pull out some of the cottony center to form troughs that will hold the goodness. Line the bread with Provolone, then make a blanket of overlapping meats. Add veggies, and drizzle with oil and vine-gar. Garnish as desired.

Set the Scene ❧❧❧❧❧❧

This is an all-American movie, set during the bicentennial year, so it's full of stars and stripes. Break out your red-white-and-blue chip dish. Then, serve your guests a platter of Italian hoagies—and, hey, why bother with plates or napkins when you can just toss them towels? Proper attire? Hoodies. For dessert? Rocky mentions doughnuts and cupcakes, but he also drinks a glass of raw eggs, so break out the frozen custard, if you want. For our purposes, we like to serve each guest a pair of chocolate turtles, a tribute to Rocky's pets.

While You're Watching...

★ Rocky's dog, Butkus, was Stallone's dog in real life. The turtles in the film are named Cuff and Link.

★ The scenes of *Rocky* running through Philadelphia were all shot guerilla-style, without extras or permits, and you can see passersby look at him curiously.

Opposite: **Rocky on the steps of the Philadelphia Museum of Art** | *Above:* **Apollo Creed (Carl Weathers) and Rocky**

ANNIE HALL (1977)

Menu

NEW YORK DELI

Brooklyn Cocktail

New York Deli Sandwich Tray

"Aware" Salad

REPARE YOURSELF FOR NEW YORK AND LOS ANGELES IN THE 1970s—Bohemian style, VW bugs, analyst jokes, and groovy parties. Woody Allen's award-winning romantic comedy takes us into the world of Alvy Singer, a stand-up comedian from New York who falls for an aspiring singer from Chippewa Falls, Wisconsin, named Annie Hall (Diane Keaton). As he reflects on their relationship, the film flashes across his past marriages, combining nostalgia and neurosis to hilarious effect—Allen's specialty.

Quirky and innovative (Allen won an Academy Award for Best Director), *Annie Hall* is also a great food film: It opens with young Alvy at the kitchen table, attempting to eat a bowl of tomato soup that sloshes around in his bowl because the family home is situated under the Coney Island roller coaster. Later, he and Annie cavort with live lobsters in the Hamptons. Near the end, Alvy heads to Hollywood to surprise Annie and stops for a meal at an A-list vegetarian joint called the Source, an actual—and influential—restaurant at the time.

Inspired by the film's bicoastal plot, we pair traditional New York deli sandwiches (think Katz's) with an iconic sprout salad, as a nod to "health food" trends of the 1960s and '70s. The cocktail, a dark and spirituous Brooklyn, may or may not be the same cocktail that Alvy's second wife lifts from a party tray early in the movie. Like hers, this one is crimson and served in a rocks glass. Its taste is bittersweet, like the film itself.

Opposite: **Diane Keaton and Woody Allen**

Brooklyn Cocktail

The Brooklyn Cocktail is a cousin to the Manhattan, one of five cocktails named after the boroughs of New York City. While similar in inflection, since it contains whiskey and vermouth, the Brooklyn adds a luxurious cherry flavor from Maraschino liqueur as well as depth from amaro. Originally Amer Picon, a bitter French aperitif, was called for. But since this is not available in the United States, we use Ramazzotti. A must-try for fans of the Manhattan.

2 ounces rye whiskey

1 ounce dry vermouth

¼ ounce Luxardo Maraschino Liqueur

¼ ounce amaro (like Ramazzotti)

Lemon twist, for garnish

Stir ingredients with ice and strain into a chilled cocktail glass. Twist the lemon peel over the drink to express the oil, then drop the peel into the cocktail.

New York Deli Sandwich Tray

Visit your best purveyor of deli meats for pastrami and corned beef. Then set about making a fabulous sandwich tray. Below are all the fixings for a terrific New York–style deli bar. If you're keeping this tray kosher, remember not to serve dairy. We like to use pumpernickel and rye bread, but you could also prepare these sandwiches on slider rolls and warm them in the oven before serving. Don't forget toothpicks to hold these sammies together.

SERVES 4 TO 6

1 loaf pumpernickel

1 loaf marble rye

1 pound pastrami, thinly sliced

1 pound corned beef, thinly sliced

1 jar sauerkraut, well drained

1 small red onion, thinly sliced

Spicy brown mustard

Horseradish

Assemble the sandwiches using a mix of the breads for color and interest. Cut each sandwich in half, and secure it with a toothpick. Arrange the halves on a serving tray, alongside kosher dills and additional condiments in bowls.

"Sun is bad for you. Everything our parents said was good is bad. Sun, milk, red meat . . . college." —ALVY SINGER

"Aware" Salad (PHOTO ON PAGE 219)

The Source restaurant on the Sunset Strip was a vegetarian oasis during the 1970s, and it appears in the second half of Annie Hall, when Alvy tries to reconnect with Annie in Los Angeles. Seated on the restaurant's sunny patio, he orders a lunch of "alfalfa sprouts and a plate of mashed yeast." In its day, the Source—owned by Father Yod (a.k.a. Jim Baker)—was a hub for healthy eaters, yogis, and famous actors. This recipe is an adaptation of the restaurant's signature salad.

SERVES 4

For the dressing

2 cloves garlic, minced

4 to 5 basil leaves, sliced into ribbons

1 teaspoon salt

1 tablespoon Dijon mustard

3 tablespoons fresh lemon juice (about 1 lemon)

1 tablespoon rice vinegar or light-colored vinegar

⅓ cup extra-virgin olive oil

For the salad

1 large head of romaine lettuce or salad greens, washed and loosely torn

1 carrot, shredded

1 beet, well-scrubbed and grated

1 cucumber, thinly sliced

2 celery ribs, chopped

1 cup shredded red cabbage

1 red bell pepper, cored and sliced into thin strips

¼ cup raw sunflower seeds

¼ cup pine nuts

1 avocado, peeled and sliced

Alfalfa sprouts, for garnish

1 to 2 tablespoons nutritional yeast, for garnish

For the dressing: Combine the garlic, basil, and salt together—a mortar and pestle works well for this, or you can drop the ingredients into a bowl and use a spoon to mash the garlic and basil up against the sides so that they release their oils. Stir in mustard, lemon juice, and vinegar. Whisk in olive oil, pouring it in slowly and whisking vigorously to combine.

To make the salad: Toss all of the ingredients in a large bowl with the dressing. Taste and add another squeeze of lemon juice or an additional pinch of salt, if needed. Top with sprouts and nutritional yeast, or serve a dish of the yeast alongside as a topper.

Opposite: **Woody Allen and Diane Keaton**

Set the Scene ▰▰▰▰▰

To highlight elements in the movie, use red geraniums as a centerpiece, serve white wine with ice cubes, and pop in a red light bulb to set the mood, as Alvy does during his seduction scene. A white shag rug would not be out of place, nor would blousy shirts and chunky beads—for both men and women. We like to start off an *Annie Hall* party with mugs of tomato soup—a nod to young Alvy in the opening scene—then set out a sandwich tray and pickles. Serve the salad after the sandwiches, when Alvy visits the Source.

While You're Watching...

★ Annie Hall had a huge influence on American fashion with her baggy chinos, dark vest, man's tie, and rumpled hat. Costume designer Ruth Morley worked with Keaton's personal style to complete Annie's signature look.

★ What's a VPL? Listen for it when Alvy and Annie attend a record producer's party in Los Angeles. It's just one of the funny phrases Allen coined in this film, along with "I lurve you, I luff you."

★ Look for appearances by Christopher Walken (Annie's brother), Paul Simon (smarmy music executive), and Jeff Goldblum (confused California partygoer).

THE BIG CHILL [1983]

Menu

CHILLING WITH BFFs

Scotch on the Rocks

Apple Pie

A FUNERAL FOR A FRIEND WHO COMMITTED suicide is the setup for one of the great ensemble cast films of all time. Now in their thirties, a cadre of once-radical college friends gathers for a few days to not just reminisce but recast their lives. Harold (Kevin Kline) and Sarah (Glenn Close) are the well-off couple who play host to their college friends: emotionally scarred drug addict Nick (William Hurt), horny journalist Michael (Jeff Goldblum), baby-crazed lawyer Meg (Mary Kay Place), TV actor Sam (Tom Berenger), frustrated housewife Karen (JoBeth Williams), and their dead friend Alex's young girlfriend, Chloe (Meg Tilly). By turns gut-wrenching and hilarious, director Lawrence Kasdan's script with Barbara Benedek is a masterpiece of humor, intrigue, and character development.

The film's most famous scene takes place in the kitchen, when the friends put away dinner dishes and dance to "Ain't Too Proud to Beg," by the Temptations. With a Motown-heavy soundtrack featuring greats like Marvin Gaye and Aretha Franklin, *The Big Chill* is among the top movies about friendship to watch with old pals. Break out the Scotch, and bake a killer pie!

William Hurt, Meg Tilly, and Jeff Goldblum

Scotch on the Rocks

What is more relaxing than sitting around with friends and pouring sips from a good bottle over hours of conversation? Scotch on the rocks calls for just one key detail: decent ice. Toss out the freezer-burned chunks, and make a fresh batch. We like to go with one large cube on a good scotch, or a few drops of water to help open the flavors. Although we love them, we avoid peaty Scotches for a group. Choose a high-land instead or something more universally palatable, such as Glenmorangie.

2 ounces Scotch

1 ice cube per glass

Pour Scotch over ice into your sturdiest low tumblers.

"Amazing tradition. They throw a great party for you on the one day they know you can't come." —MICHAEL GOLD

Apple Pie (PHOTO ON PAGE 224)

Not surprising for a film about a gathering of friends, there are many kitchen scenes in The Big Chill, *and simple comfort fare for the group prevails. In one scene, Sarah and Meg make apple pie together, which gave us the inspiration for this simple menu. We like to take this classic recipe and add a twist of spice from Angostura bitters. It doesn't hurt that this is a great companion to Scotch. Note: This makes a double-crusted 10-inch pie.*

SERVES 6 TO 8

For the pie crust

3 cups all-purpose white flour

1 teaspoon salt

2½ sticks (1¼ cups) cold unsalted butter, cut into ¼-inch pats

1 tablespoon sour cream

5 tablespoons ice-cold water, plus more as needed

For the filling and top

2 tablespoons fresh lemon juice

5 to 6 apples, peeled, cored, and diced (preferably a mix of red and green)

⅓ cup sugar (preferably raw), plus more for sprinkling on top

2 tablespoons all-purpose white flour

¼ teaspoon ground cinnamon

⅛ teaspoon ground nutmeg

6 dashes bitters (Angostura or Bittercube Jamaican #1)

1 egg

1 teaspoon sea salt (flake), for garnish

1 teaspoon raw sugar, for garnish

To make the crust in a food processor: Combine flour and salt in a large bowl. In the bowl of a food processor, add ⅔ of the flour mixture and the butter. Pulse until combined and there is no dry flour. Add remaining flour and pulse until dough starts to break up. Transfer it back to the large bowl, add sour cream, then begin adding ice-cold water a tablespoon at a time until the dough just barely hangs together. Work the dough into a ball with a spatula. Divide in half, cover with cling wrap, and refrigerate for 2 hours.

To make the crust by hand: Start with a large chilled bowl to keep the butter cold. In it, combine the flour, salt, chopped butter, and sour cream. Use a pastry cutter to work the butter down into pea-size lumps. Then begin adding ice-cold water a tablespoon at a time as you stir with a spatula.

Keep your hands out of the bowl so that the butter remains as cold as possible. When the dough becomes shaggy and just barely hangs together, use your hands to form two balls. They will be clumpy and crack—fear not. Wrap them well in plastic wrap, and get them into the fridge as fast as possible.

To make the pie: In a medium bowl, combine lemon juice and apples, coating the apples. In a small bowl, mix together sugar, flour, cinnamon, nutmeg, and bitters. Sprinkle the mixture over apples, and combine using a spatula or your hands.

To assemble, preheat the oven to 375°F. Roll doughs into two equal rounds and place the bottom dough in the pie tin. Add the filling and your second round of dough on top. Pinch the edges closed.

In a small bowl, whisk the egg briefly to break up the yolk. Brush the egg on top of the pie, and sprinkle salt flakes and raw sugar. With a knife, cut several slits in the crust to let steam escape. Set the pie on a parchment-lined baking tray to catch any drips, then put the pie in the oven. Set the timer for 1 hour.

After 15 minutes of baking, cover the pie edge with 2 to 3 inches of tinfoil so it doesn't over-brown. Bake another 45 minutes, or until apples are tender and the top crust is brown. Let the pie cool before serving.

JoBeth Williams, Kevin Kline, William Hurt, and Glenn Close

Set the Scene ◄◄◄◄◄

Prepare to get comfortable. Blankets, pillows, a pitcher of water. This is a mellow movie—after all, it is called *The Big Chill*. Pour some Scotch, set out the pie, and get ready for some great 1980s hair. If you want to serve a more filling meal, try our roast chicken (page 50) or make a big "Aware" Salad (page 220). After the movie, be sure to throw on some 1960s Motown and get everyone into the kitchen to dance and wash dishes.

While You're Watching...

★ If the actors seem comfortable together, it's because they are; they lived together for a few weeks before filming, and the day before filming they stayed together in character.

★ The character of Alex was supposed to be played by Kevin Costner, but director Lawrence Kasdan ended up cutting out the flashbacks to Alex's life. In exchange for this career blow, Kasdan offered Costner a part in his next film, *Silverado*.

★ Look for the amazing product placement scene with classic Nike running shoes.

Right: **Glenn Close and Kevin Kline**

MOONSTRUCK (1987)

Menu

LOVESTRUCK BRUNCH

Champagne Cocktail

Easy Antipasti Plate

Toad in the Hole with Sautéed Peppers

Espresso with Italian Pastries (suggested)

MOONSTRUCK WAS MADE FOR PEOPLE WHO LOVE HANGING OUT in kitchens, especially with Italian nonnas at the stove. It begins and ends with home-cooked breakfasts prepared by Rose Castorini (Olympia Dukakis) for her daughter (Cher), and most major scenes take place in a kitchen. Or an Italian restaurant. Or a specialty foods store full of low-hanging sausages. You can't watch this film without wanting to nosh on crusty bread or pour yourself a big glass of red wine. Although our menu is a re-creation of the film's final brunch scene, you could easily serve this meal for dinner.

Cher is in her prime here—dreamy and alluring. She stars as Loretta Castorini, a thirty-something widow, who lives with her parents in pre-hipster Brooklyn and manages the books for her aunt and uncle's cheese shop. When she falls in love with Ronny Cammareri (Nicolas Cage), a passionate bread baker with a screaming hot temper, there's just one problem: she's engaged to his brother! You can just imagine the drama that unfolds as she fesses up to her extended family over breakfast, after walking through the door in a red dress and red high heels.

Prepare for high comedy and stellar acting—Cher won Best Actress, Olympia Dukakis Best Supporting Actress. *Moonstruck* also snagged Best Original Screenplay. The film is as magical today as it was in the 1980s. Watch it with plenty of nosh when you need an uplifting mood changer or a romantic chill-out night.

Opposite: **A family portrait in the living room of the Castorini house**

Champagne Cocktail

Loretta Castorini and her father (Vincent Gardenia) prepare these cocktails at the kitchen table early in the film to celebrate her engagement. You'll see them drop a sugar cube into a glass of Champagne, which creates a festive plume of bubbles. Traditionally, a Champagne cocktail also includes a dash of bitters and a lemon twist, two things that build on the beautiful aroma of good bubbly. Use a Brut Champagne or Crémant (bubbly made outside of the Champagne region). This is lovely with antipasti.

1 sugar cube

1 dash Angostura bitters

4 ounces sparkling wine

Lemon twist, for garnish

Drop a sugar cube into a Champagne flute. Lightly moisten the cube with a dash of Angostura bitters. Fill the glass with sparkly, and garnish with a lemon twist on the edge of the glass.

Above: **Vincent Gardenia and Cher** | *Opposite:* **Mrs. Castorini (Olympia Dukakis) serving a plate of Toad in the Hole with peppers to her daughter**

Tips for Building an Easy Antipasti Plate

Go to a good Italian cheese shop like the one in the movie and ask for the following: a hunk of sharp Provolone, a jagged wedge of real Parmigiano Reggiano, a link of sweet or spicy soppressata, some thinly sliced mortadella, some sun-dried tomatoes in olive oil, a box of crackery breadsticks, and some juicy green olives as big as your cousin Vinny's pinkie ring.

When you get home, set everything out on a big cutting board—use a paring knife to chunk up the Parmigiano into bite-size pieces (it will taste great with the Champagne cocktail), fold the mortadella into quarters, and leave everything else whole for people to wrestle over.

Set the Scene

It's the 1980s! Think big hair, bold colors, baggy sweaters. The movie is set in an Italian neighborhood in Brooklyn. Think doilies, doilies, doilies! Break out your granny china and spritz the house with some rosewater. Then fluff the couch pillows and set out a vase full of breadsticks and a tray of Champagne glasses. Since *Moonstruck* is about fate, try to host your movie party on a full moon, and invite a friend with a tarot card deck to read everyone's fortune.

Toad in the Hole with Sautéed Peppers

Moonstruck must have been an amazing movie to shoot because there is food in just about every scene, from bagels and butter early on to a tiramisu cake that eclipses a restaurant dessert cart. There's also a great scene where Cher's character fixes a steak with a side of spaghetti—don't be afraid to sub in our Manhattan-Marinated Flank Steak (page 146) here. Toad in the Hole, in case you don't know it, goes by many names: Bird in a Nest, Egg in a Basket, and One-Eyed Jack. Scale it up or down, and serve it with an arugula salad tossed with olive oil and a splash of good balsamic.

SERVES 4

1 garlic clove, peeled and halved

2 tablespoons extra-virgin olive oil

2 red bell peppers, cored and sliced into strips

4 slices bread (rustic Italian works well)

2 to 3 tablespoons butter, softened

4 eggs

Salt and freshly ground black pepper, to taste

Fresh oregano, for garnish

Grated Parmigiano cheese, for garnish

Run a garlic clove around the surface of a large skillet or griddle, then set the skillet over medium heat. Run a few circles of olive oil around the pan. Then drop in the peppers and let them cook until they soften, about 5 to 8 minutes. Remove peppers from the pan, and set aside for later.

On a counter or flat surface, use a shot glass to make holes in the center of each bread slice. Slather the slices with butter, remove the center circles, and set the bread into the hot pan, arranging the centers around the edge.

Crack an egg into the hole of each bread slice and fry on medium or medium-low, about 2 minutes per side. You want the yolks to stay a little runny.

Top with salt and pepper, a pinch or two of oregano, and some grated cheese. Serve the peppers alongside.

"Pop, I've got news."
—LORETTA CASTORINI

"All right. Let's go into
the kitchen." —MR. CASTORINI

While You're Watching...

★ Look for the epic screen kiss between Cher and Nicolas Cage in his kitchen. It may be the best kitchen kiss on film. (Cage was twenty-two, Cher was forty.)

★ Director Norman Jewison had an eye for creating Hollywood films that were unusually artful and yet mainstream. Long before *Moonstruck*, he worked on *Fiddler on the Roof* (1971) and *Jesus Christ Superstar* (1973). Before *Moonstruck*, he directed *Agnes of God* (1985).

★ Cher's part in *Moonstruck* was first offered to Sally Field, who turned it down.

Cher and Nicolas Cage

TAKE THREE

Special Occasions and Resources

MOVIES FOR THE HOLIDAYS

Host a cocktail and cookie party with cinema, or project one of these films on your living room wall during a holiday open house. All these movies feature at least one holiday scene.

The Divorcée (page 13)
The Apartment (page 148)
Rocky (page 210)
The Big Chill (page 222)

Also: *Meet John Doe* (1941), *Holiday Inn* (1942), *Meet Me in St. Louis* (1944), *Christmas in Connecticut* (1945), *It's a Wonderful Life* (1946), *Miracle on 34th Street* (1947), *Holiday Affair* (1949), *By the Light of the Silvery Moon* (1953), *White Christmas* (1954), *A Christmas Carol* (1951), *Swiss Family Robinson* (1960), *Trading Places* (1983), *Rocky IV* (1985), *Hannah and Her Sisters* (1986)

DATE NIGHT MOVIES

Take "Netflix and chill" to new heights? These movie menus make impressive intimate suppers, or you can plan a double or triple date night.

Female (page 29)
The Thin Man (page 36)
Casablanca (page 73)
Adam's Rib (page 96)
Roman Holiday (page 119)
Guys and Dolls (page 127)
Some Like It Hot (page 140)
Annie Hall (page 216)
Moonstruck (page 230)

Also: *It Happened One Night* (1934), *The Lady Eve* (1941), *Now, Voyager* (1942), *Singin' in the Rain* (1952), *An Affair to Remember* (1957), *Doctor Zhivago* (1965), *Guess Who's Coming to Dinner* (1967)

MOVIE MENUS FOR CROWDS AND CELEBRATIONS

Planning a reunion, engagement party, anniversary bash, retirement, or graduation? Please look no further.

The Thin Man (page 36)
Dodsworth (page 53)
The Philadelphia Story (page 67)
Rope (page 88)
Sunset Boulevard (page 104)
An American in Paris (page 110)
Breakfast at Tiffany's (page 156)
The Graduate (page 180)
Funny Girl (page 189)
The Big Chill (page 222)

FAMILY FILM NIGHT

These are casual menus, good for a Sunday supper or weeknight. How about a Throwback Thursday movie night?

Chained (page 45)
Stagecoach (page 59)
The Lady from Shanghai (page 80)
Giant (page 134)
Blue Hawaii (page 164)
The Sting (page 196)
American Graffiti (page 205)

Resources

These are a few of the books, websites, films, and podcasts that inspired us during the process of writing this book. May they guide you deeper into the world of food, drink, and film.

Books

Of All the Gin Joints: Stumbling Through Hollywood History, by Mark Bailey and Edward Hemingway (Algonquin Books, 2014)

Hollywood's America: Twentieth-Century America Through Film, edited by Steven Mintz and Randy W. Roberts (Wiley-Blackwell, 2010)

Food in the Movies (Second Edition), by Steve Zimmerman (McFarland, 2010)

Martini, Straight Up: The Classic American Cocktail, by Lowell Edmunds (Johns Hopkins, 1998)

Websites

www.tcm.com
www.imdb.com
www.filmsite.org
www.alcohollywood.com
www.punchdrink.com
www.eatdrinkfilms.com

Multimedia

The Story of Film: An Odyssey (fifteen-part documentary, by Mark Cousins)

You Must Remember This (podcast, by Karina Longworth)

Acknowledgments

Like a film, a book is a collaborative effort. We're grateful to Turner Classic Movies and Running Press for providing us with this rich project. Special thanks to our editor, Cindy De La Hoz, and to book designer Susan Van Horn for their guidance and enthusiasm; to Amy Williams, our agent; to photographer Andrew Purcell, stylist Carrie Purcell, and the super team at Forty North Studio in New York. Many friends and neighbors joined us for movie nights and recipe testing: special thanks to Emily Geddes for her period suggestions on table settings. To our parents, and to Tenaya's partner, Todd, thank you for your support—for enduring the sticky countertops, the broken glasses, the many evenings spent cooking with laptops propped on toaster ovens.

Index